Our Father

JAMES HARKESS

Our Father

A New Catholic's
Daily Conversation
with God

with a Foreword by
Lord Longford

ST PAULS

ST PAULS
London SW1P 1EP, United Kingdom
Maynooth, Co Kildare, Ireland

© ST PAULS (UK) 1998

ISBN 085439 529 6

Set by TuKan, High Wycombe
Produced in the EC
Printed by The Guernsey Press Co. Ltd, Guernsey, C. I.

ST PAULS is an activity of the priests and brothers of the
Society of St Paul who proclaim the Gospel through the media
of social communication

*With love
to my wonderful wife Valerie,
and our three children,
Alison, Josephine and Alexander*

'…He who hears my word
and believes him who sent me
has eternal life:
He does not come into judgement
but has passed from death to life.'
John 5:24

Our Father

Our Father which are in Heaven.
Hallowed be thy name.
Thy Kingdom come.
Thy will be done on earth, as it is in Heaven.
Give us this day our daily bread.
And forgive us our trespasses
as we forgive those that trespass against us.
Lead us not into temptation.
But deliver us from evil. Amen

Pater Noster

Pater Noster, qui es in chaelis,
Sanctificetur nomen tuum.
Adveniat regnum tuum.
Fiat volentas tua sicut in caelo et in terra.
Panem nostrum supersubstantialem da nobis hodie
Et dimitte nobis debita nostra,
sicut et nos dimittimus debitoribus nostris.
Et ne nos inducas intentationem: sed libera nos a malo.
Amen

Let us pray to thee Our Father
Every evening of our life
May we ask thee, love thee, hear thee
Know thy Kingdom has arrived.

In pure love of thee our Saviour
Might our commune be direct
Glory to thy triune Godhead
On earth thy two-fold Will perfect.

Grant us daily all thy succour
Thank thee always for thy good.
Seven sacraments adorn us
These, O Lord, are all our food.

Trespass must we: sin is in us
Are we forgiven? Let us know.
Intercede, O Blessed Mary
But first we must forgive our foe.

Jesus prevent the anti-Christ
From taking o'er our story
For thou alone are highest
In thy Father's glory. Amen

Contents

Foreword

Our Father is one of those books that needs to be published, and who better to do so than ST PAULS who last year celebrated their fiftieth anniversary as publishers. The Society of St Paul, under whose auspices they function has been instrumental in spreading the Gospel widely and well for 83 years.

The author James Harkess has set out to analyse and interpret the greatest prayer of all time, the *Pater Noster*, the Lord's Prayer, that Christ taught his original disciples that they might teach it to the world. In this endeavour I believe he has succeeded. So far as I know and I have been studying and reading the New Testament on a daily basis for over 60 years, this is the first treatment of the prayer which I have encountered which draws attention to its purpose petition by petition. In the author's view our Lord meant it to be a framework on which all Christian prayers should be based. In what to me is a useful and a colourful phrase he describes Jesus' prayer as 'a vehicle seldom if ever driven to its full capacity'.

With some skill he proceeds over the chapters to clothe Christ's beautiful frame by way of extended prayers to fit each petition. In this way is built the basis for what he calls our 'daily conversation with God'. Furthermore, the Lord's prayer is patently designed for daily use by the people of God in their private devotion (quite aside from when it is said as part of Church liturgy). One has only to pray the fourth petition – 'Give us this day our daily bread' – to realise it is so.

I was not in any way instrumental in the conversion of James to the Catholic Church which occurred a few years ago, although we have more recently discussed it together. The book's subtitle in which James refers to himself as a 'New Catholic' is in itself of some considerable interest to others. This will be so for all those who take this path during the course of their lives on earth. My wife and myself were received into the Catholic Church over 50 years ago and my eight children in due course.

In wishing the book well, I hope it is widely read and enjoyed not only by Catholics but all Christians as well as those who are not. I cannot exaggerate its value.

Frank Longford
House of Lords
London, 26 September 1997

Preface

I have greatly enjoyed writing this book, and hope that some of this joy is shared by you when you read it. I am neither a priest nor a religious nor a Doctor of Divinity. As a lawyer I will not say 'I come with clean hands', rather as a layman hoping to impart something of my study and enthusiasm, to you the reader.

The Introduction sets the scene, which is the broad canvas of prayer, with particular reference to the most important prayer of all creation – the Lord's Prayer, more affectionately known throughout Christendom as the Our Father. Since it is in my view, having lived with it and thought about it for two years and more, the framework for all other prayer and devotion to God, the task became greater than I had at first imagined. It also became more exciting that I had ever conceived.

Next come the seven petitions of the prayer in chapters one to seven, which are arranged in this way. After the title of the petition as given by Christ to his twelve disciples, comes an analysis or interpretation of its meaning (wherever possible but at not too great length or the work would be vast which is not the intention). I have tried to give illustrative reference, by means of Scripture or early Church Authorities to the points I make.

A further section deals with what I call 'extended prayers' to the petition. The idea is that by using them it is possible to follow a pattern of prayer on a regular basis, enlarging in a purely logical way on the framework or skeleton of each petition. I am convinced that this is the way in which Christ meant the prayer to be used, and I believe the early Fathers support this view.

Each chapter ends with a brief résumé of the extended prayers, pausing for comment upon them where I feel it may be of interest. Inevitably there are personal anecdotes and sketches, sometimes bearing on my life or people I have met, which I trust will not upset or divert more than for a moment; even better if they might amuse or interest.

Chapter 8 deals with the *Doxology*. This is about the only thing which upsets me as a New Catholic, and I say so, in praise of my former adherence to the Anglican communion!

The work concludes with the chapter entitled 'Amen', which is self-explanatory, and delves deeper into some vexed questions of dogma and faith. All are connected in one way or another with praying the Our Father and our daily conversation with God. I hope it may stimulate us to think more deeply into serious issues that affect Christians today.

Finally there is an Index, which I trust will be helpful. My wife Valerie taught me many years ago that no book, other than one of fiction, was of any use at all, without an index. May God bless and praise her for her wisdom!

I have sub-titled this book 'A New Catholic's Daily Conversations with God', which may require some explanation.

Why a 'New Catholic'? Is it for example anything akin to 'New Labour'. No it is not, and that does not mean I disapprove of New Labour, I do not. It means simply this. At the age of sixty-plus I decided to take the plunge and do what I should have done many years earlier: become a Catholic. I do not mean that everyone should do the same. It is obviously a very personal decision. If anyone would be interested to know, I would like to tell them why, in some detail, but not in this book. It was interesting to me that at about the same time as I converted to Catholicism so did one of my godsons and his parents. This news was unknown to me until after the event, as my news was to them. I was asked by one of the nuns present at my reception near Cape Town, why I had decided 'at such a late age' to change to Catholicism – I told her without hesitation – 'if it had not been for King Henry VIII of England, I would, like most Britons, have been one anyway'.

A New Catholic merely means someone who has recently converted to, or to give its proper term 'been received' into the Roman Catholic Church, after a due period of thought and instruction. I believe it is relevant to mention this at the outset of a book of this kind, so the reader can better understand certain feelings or positions if and when they arise. Just as some Christians (fewer and fewer I hope!) could not abide Catholic viewpoints or dogma, there may well be others born of Catholic parents and who have grown up accepting the Catholic faith from a very early life, who may be surprised at some of the distinctions I draw or conclusions I come to. At least I have put my cards on the table, face-up, in the hope it will assist all readers, Christians (Protestant or Catholic) as well as Muslims, and others, and which may well include agnostics and atheists (see chapter 9) to follow my reasoning from the viewpoint of truth. If one wants to share a new-found joy with others, why be afraid to state your case and your personal convictions? If there are those who would take issue with what you say, that is their privilege, but they cannot say they have not been informed. If, on the other hand, what you say makes some sense, perhaps it will be able to provide some help as well. We have God given free-will and as I stress, the choice is ours.

I would like to thank my publishers, St Pauls, particularly Fr Sebastian Karamvelil, Fr Les Pruszynski and Andrew Tulloch for their patience and understanding towards me, in the production of this book – as well as introducing me to the splendid work done worldwide by the Society of St Paul.

I shall always be grateful for the encouragement of my friend, Frank Longford, and for his kindness in writing the Foreword. From such a devoted and courageous man of God I count it an honour.

My loving wife, Valerie, who has supported my labour through its entire progress deserves and has my living gratitude.

Introduction

C hristian prayer is talking to God. It is communion with God. It should mean, for he or she who prays, that they engage in a unique and wonderful conversation with the Almighty on a regular basis. Hence the title of this book, which is an attempt to help all who strive for holiness to come so much nearer to that state.

I came to realise that the most practical way of achieving that state was to offer a planned prayer –based entirely on the greatest prayer of all time – *The Lord's Prayer*. It seemed to me this all-embracing vehicle designed for mankind by the Son of God himself, is seldom driven to its full and wonderful capacity. The very origin of the prayer (as recorded by St Luke, cf Lk 11:1) is its handing over to Christ's disciples following the request of one of them 'Lord teach us how to pray'.

Since everyone of us who professes to be Christian is bidden to proclaim God's word, I realised that a duty lay on me to use my talents in this direction. Four brief quotations will for the moment suffice.

'Woe to me if I do not proclaim the Gospel', St Paul's words in 1 Cor 9:16; and 'The mission of Evangelization is an essential part of the Church', Pope John Paul II.

'Go into all the world', Mk 16:15; and 'Go therefore

and make disciples of all nations' Mt 28:19; the words of Christ himself in the gospels.

A few years ago I began to help myself to pray in a more meaningful way, with considerable assistance, I hasten to add, from the Holy Spirit, so that I now feel confident in passing on a recipe or formula which has begun to enrich my spiritual life, in the hope it may do the same for those who follow it.

I would like to declare an interest at the outset by saying that four years ago I decided to take religious instruction with a view to being received into the Catholic faith. I duly became a Roman Catholic in May 1995. This declaration is in no way meant to deter let alone upset those readers who are not Catholics, nor even those who doubt the Christian faith or are agnostics. Far from it; indeed, it is declared so as to explain a bent towards Catholic liturgy and dogma, sometimes mingled with that of my former Anglican upbringing. Naturally the change from one Christian church to another was made in joy and from a long personal conviction, but I trust that all who believe in our Lord Jesus Christ, or even those who would care to find him, might in some way be refreshed and interested by this guide to prayer.

There could be as many definitions of prayer as there are people in San Marino (which for the record is about 25,000). I give you a very few of my favourites, and in no way apologise that others appear from time to time in the pages of this book:

> For me prayer is a surge of the heart; it is a simple look turned towards Heaven. It is a cry of recognition and of love, embracing both trial and joy.
>
> (St Thérèse of Lisieux)

and

> The wonder of prayer is revealed beside the well where we come seeking water there, Christ comes to meet every human being. It is he who first seeks us

and asks us for a drink. Jesus thirsts; his asking arises from the depths of God's desire for us. Whether we realise it or not, prayer is the encounter of God's thirst with ours. God thirsts that we may thirst for him.   St Augustine

I pray that you may have the power to comprehend, with all the saints, what is the breadth and length and height and depth, and to know the love of Christ that surpasses knowledge, so that you may be filled with all the fullness of God. Now to him who by the power at work within us is able to accomplish abundantly far more than all we can ask or imagine, to him be glory in the church and in Christ Jesus to all generations, forever and ever. Amen.   (Eph 3:18-21)

In the same vein there are countless prayers of great holiness and beauty, that it does wonders for us as Christians (and also if we are not!) to know, study or recite them.

The Our Father, the subject of this book, is the fount of all prayer. But arising from it, or flowing beside it as tributaries to the stream of life, are so many others. The Jesus Prayer, 'Lord Jesus Christ, Son of God, have mercy on me a sinner...'; Mary's prayers, The Magnificat, and her *Fiat* 'Behold I am the handmaid of the Lord. Let it be done (Fiat) according to your word', – all these are poignant examples.

My talents have always been artistic or aesthetic rather than scientific or practical. They encompass appreciation of fine music, an interest in philosophy and politics, a desire to impart through writing and speech; they are decidedly weak in handiwork, ball games, pure science or physics. It would therefore go against the grain to present such a personal and sensitive subject as prayer under the format of 'DIY'. Indeed I am ashamed to say it was only a few years ago that I learned these initials stood for 'Do it yourself'. Having said this, private prayer is something so especially personal, being a gift that can only be returned to Him or shared with Him, by the supplicant. It is therefore something which you can only 'do yourself'. But it can be done according to a plan; it should be done as comprehensively as possible; it ought to be a natural and beautiful experience; it would probably embrace elements of praise, love, thanks, petition, as well as listening.

Of course private prayer should never be reduced to a meaningless routine, pursued without care or recited thoughtlessly like a wound-up pupil desperate to learn by rote the many stanzas of a poem set for homework the day before. God deserves better than that and so does his petitioner. But if there is no plan worked out in advance, no agenda for this daily talk with God, then even though he will understand such human failure, a great deal will have been lost, including much needed enrichment of the soul.

There is much truth in the old adage 'practice makes perfect'. In many respects we learn to pray by praying. In other respects it is Jesus who teaches us to pray by his own example. St Luke tells us how Jesus 'spent the night in prayer to God', and again how he went up into the hills by himself to pray. Before his passion and death he went to the Mount of Olives, encouraged the apostles to pray, knelt down and prayed himself. During his agony he prayed intensely. Only once when requested by the disciples: 'Lord teach us to pray' (Lk 11:1) 'did he give them the simplest and the deepest content of his prayer: the Our Father.

I believe the Lord's Prayer is a diving exhortation, the power of which will never be surpassed: and the single most important object of this book is to promote and champion this fact.

If we accept the historicity of the well-recorded sayings of Christ, then the import of these particular few dozen words is monumental (but it is worth noting that this historicity is a question of considerable delicacy and not one that appears to have any solution that is acceptable to all – at the very least we as Catholics can say that the

Church guarantees their divine inspiration). But they cannot, should not be treated in isolation, and in my view ought to be read in conjunction with what has been called the 'priestly prayer'.

If the Our Father was given to the world in the earlier part of Jesus' three-year ministry, we know the priestly prayer – also known, with reason as the 'prayer of the hour of Jesus' – came in the final hours of our Saviour's life, immediately before his betrayal in the Garden of Gethsemane (Jn 17:1ff).

The beautiful and emotive words of the later prayer occupy the entire seventeenth chapter of St John's Gospel.

Beginning – 'Father the hour has come...', this priestly prayer provides complete corroboration for the Our Father of two or more years before.[1] The *Catechism of the Catholic Church* (para. 2750) has to say:

> His priestly prayer fulfils, from within, the great petitions of the Lord's prayer...

It is small wonder that some writers and commentators throughout the ages dare not accept the 'Gospel truth' of much of the New Testament, and certainly not the priestly prayer of Jesus!

In discourse in Rome in March 1979, Pope John Paul II elaborated further on the importance of Christ's prayer and his words are very apt.

> All that can and must be said to the Father is contained in these seven requests, which we all know by heart. There is such a simplicity in them that even a child can learn them, and also such a depth that a whole life can be spent meditating on each of them.[2]

The Pope continued his treatise by pointing to the need for prayer – through the perfect medium of the Our Father – to be all-embracing. 'Everything must find its way into our "conversation with God", even things of which we are ashamed or which burden us, as this demolishes the barrier which sin and evil may have raised between us and God.'

Christ taught us his prayer, through the disciples two thousand years ago. Christ's vicar – as Catholics sometimes call the pope – helped us to interpret and use the prayer in 1979. It is safe to say that two thousand years from now the subject will still be open for discussion and interpretation. It may however be a few millennia before the Pontiff's concluding words on that occasion can be matched, for their wonder and significance. 'Prayer' he said, 'is the sacrifice of our lips'. It is like desire for God, as St Ignatius of Antioch writes: spring water that murmurs within us and says: "Come to the Father" (cf *CCC* 1011)'.

Once we have discovered the essentials of praying, it becomes fruitful to explore the detailed path to take in our daily habit, and this I suggest in the seven chapters of the book – each one based on the petitions in the prayer. What are these essentials? In the New Testament most of the basic tenets of prayer are to be found. First, in the gospels there are many references to the tradition of prayer. Of the fifty or so, perhaps six would suffice.

In the first of these Jesus speaks of simplicity and sincerity in praying 'And whenever you pray, do not be like the hypocrites; for they love to stand and pray in the synagogues and at the street corners, so that they may be seen by others.' 'Shut the door and pray to your Father who is in secret; and your Father who sees in secret will reward you.' He goes on to urge us '...when you are praying, do not heap up empty phrases for your Father knows what you need before you ask him' (Mt 6:5ff). And then, 'Pray then in this way: Our Father...' According to Matthew, our Lord repeats himself – here for a purpose and certainly not out of vanity – and after the words of the *Pater Noster* are ended by 'Amen', verses 14 and 15 continue: 'for if you forgive others their trespasses, your heavenly Father will also forgive you...'. I will refer again to this passage in chapter 5.

In St Mark's Gospel there is no full mention of the Lord's Prayer or how it came about. There is partial reference to it in chapter 12 verse 24: 'So I tell you, whatever you ask for in prayer, believe that you have received it, and it will be yours... whenever you stand praying, forgive, if you have anything against anyone; so that your Father in Heaven may also forgive you your trespasses.'

Again the warning follows: if not, neither will you be forgiven. Hence the vital importance of the tradition of forgiveness through prayer, the second of the three traditional essentials in the gospels that I mention.

The third, again I chose from St Mark's Gospel. One of the scribes brought before Jesus his son, who had a dumb spirit or was subject to fits (Mk 9:14ff). Our Lord's miracle in curing the child before his disciples, teaches the doctrine of faith and prayer through the same, which operates in surrender to God's will 'If you can believe, all things are possible to him who believes' (verse 23).

The fourth tradition of importance is surely that all prayer should be directed to the Trinity, or offered in Christ's name. The Fourth Gospel has three references to this need (Jn 14:13, 15:16, 16:23). In the first of these Jesus says to his disciples: '...and whatsoever you shall ask in my name, that will I do, that the Father may be glorified in the Son'.[3] In other words, believe and pray to the effect that Christ has secured for man a new access to the Father in prayer. And to complete the Trinity, John recalls Jesus saying, 'And I will pray the Father, and he shall give you another comforter that he may abide with you forever' (Jn 14:16).

Our Lord prayed to his father in Heaven, as an example to man so to do, when in dire spiritual conflict, even as he foretold his own death:

Now my soul is troubled. And what should I say – 'Father, save me from this hour?' No, it is for this reason that I have come to this hour (Jn 12:27).

God the Father instantly heard him, as he will hear us. This then, the fifth tenet.

A simple direct sixth tenet, that of thanksgiving is found in Matthew 26:27, when at the Last Supper Jesus 'took a cup and and after giving thanks, he gave it to them, saying, "Drink from it, all of you..."' and again at the feeding of the five thousand, he '...took the loaves and when he had given thanks, he distributed them to the disciples...'. Thanksgiving is at the cornerstone of the Lord's Prayer.

Prayer can be contemplative as well as vocal and direct, and time is well taken to pause for such contemplation. I will deal further with this in the chapter on the first petition... 'Hallowed by Thy name' (chapter 1).

St Teresa of Jesus refers to such prayer as 'Mental prayer' and writes that it is 'a close sharing between friends' and 'means taking time frequently to be alone with Him who we know loves us.'[4] The *Catechism of the Catholic Church* (para 2711ff) likens entering into contemplative prayer to 'entering the Eucharistic liturgy, when we gather up the heart and awaken our faith in order to enter into the presence of him who awaits us'.

It enables Christ 'to dwell in our hearts through faith' that we be 'grounded in love' (Eph 3:16-17). It is given in silence, though as I believe, and elaborate upon in chapter 1, it can be both received and answered.

Prayer is a gift of grace for which –when we pray – we should find a space to thank God. It requires effort, not only in time, but more importantly in study, research and in the use of our intellect. Often when we are tired or have other preoccupations it takes discipline to address God in a true and meaningful way; but wondrous is the inspiration of the Holy Spirit on such occasions.

To those who prize production and profit, prayer is far from being unproductive or unprofitable! Others treat prayer as escapism whereas it is the very opposite since God is the ultimate reality.

According to the Holy Father: 'through all prayer one

must proclaim glory. Prayer is always an *opus gloriae* and man is the priest of all creation.'[5]

There are some who no longer pray or who only do so in extremis – and I use the word here not only to mean in fear of death, but also when anything fearful or seriously worrying confronts them. The reason for these lapsed supplicants (and probably lapsed Christians too) is often that they feel their prayers are not answered, or fail to understand the way in which they are answered. May it help if I proffer the words of the writer George Meredith (1880–1926): 'whoever rises from prayer a better man', he says, 'his prayer is answered', God, whether our Creator, redeemer or comforter, hears our prayers. If we hold fast to our faith and believe what he himself has told us in this regard we can be certain of that. Once God has heard us he becomes our everloving respondent. Imagine ourself as the one who makes the call. It is direct dialling, toll free and the line is open twenty-four hours a day. The only other mystery is that the recipient know in advance that you will call him; moreover he knows what you will ask of him or say to him. So why bother in the first place asks the cynic? Because the caller has free will, given him/her by God. Our Lord needs to hear the contents of the call all the more since the free will given to us is ours to exercise not His to command.

Pope John Paul II puts it this way: 'In prayer then the true protagonist is God.' (He underlines that sentence – as he often does in his writing when he wishes to emphasise a point.) 'We begin to pray', he continues, 'believing that it is our own initiative that compels us to do so. Instead we learn that it is always God's initiative within us. This initiative restores in us our true humanity… our true dignity.'[6]

In whatever form of prayer – vocal (be it liturgical or personal) or contemplative prayer, there is bound to be distraction. Whenever this occurs we should turn back to our heartfelt love of God, in the humility which is felt between the consecration and consumption of his body and blood at the Eucharistic feast. At that time above all others our hearts and minds are attuned to the glorious union of ourselves with our Saviour – present with him, in him, through his body and blood. I believe that in prayer we can contemplate the sacrament of the Eucharist, without of course experiencing it. In a different way we can pray for our spouse and thank God for the sacrament of Marriage, whilst at the same time contemplating the joy of the union of one flesh (body and soul) which Christ blessed in his first miracle at Cana. The best answer to distraction is vigilance. The last day may be yesterday, any day, today. The bridegroom comes in the middle of the night; the light that must not be extinguished is that of faith. 'Come' my heart says, 'seek his face' (Ps 27:8).

The Acts of the Apostles form an excellent link between the gospels and the epistles. Here the Apostolic Church puts into perspective Christ's teaching on prayer. There are several references to the Church leaders being men of prayer; the main examples being Peter, Paul and Silas.

> The father of Publius lay sick of a fever... to whom Paul entered into and prayed, and laid his hands on him and healed him (Acts 28:8).

Likewise the Pauline epistles show us the power and beauty of St Paul's written words to the faithful of the early Church, often with emphasis on the strength and reward of prayer: 'put on the whole armour of God, that ye may be able to stand against the wiles of the devil'. Later, Paul says we should 'stand with our loins girt... with truth... taking the shield of faith... the helmet of salvation and the sword of the Spirit, which is the Word of God, praying always...' (Eph 6:11ff) prayer here being as a gift of the Holy Spirit.

It is not only from the Bible and the New Testament in particular that students of prayer can seek knowledge. Clerics, theologians and lay people alike should seek it from every source. A theologian of much wisdom and who has helped me by his writing – unhappily I never met him – was Mgr Ronald Knox, who died in 1957. Knox came from an Anglican family; his father being Bishop of Manchester in the 1910s. After a brilliant career at Oxford where he graduated and was ordained into the Church of England, he became a fellow of Trinity College as well as Chaplain. In 1917 he was received into the Catholic Church and later ordained – becoming Chaplain to Oxford University in 1926. He undertook a translation of the Vulgate edition of the Bible which was completed in 1949. His numerous writing included detective thrillers, essays and religious works. When lying ill and near to death, and asked by a friend if he would care to listen to a reading from the New Testament, Knox is reputed to have said, 'no, but awfully jolly of you to suggest it'.

Ronald Knox said much that is edifying about the theology of prayer. He believed that when man is in a state of grace, his or her prayer can obtain satisfaction 'for temporary punishment due to sin' as the language of the time would have it. These prayers moreover can win merit by an increase in grace, since prayer moves God to show mercy. He taught that prayer brings both spiritual refreshment as well as religious knowledge. It also produces fear, joy and a desire for God and makes the three virtues – faith, hope and love – more dynamic in the life of the supplicant. In other words he was adamant that through prayer on a continual and regular basis, could come a progressive union with God – a gradual transformation into Christ. The ends of prayer he saw as praise, love, adoration, thanksgiving, propitiation, petition, and importantly, listening. Prayer, to Knox, was a necessary means to salvation.

Certainly the Lord's Prayer is the ideal model which Knox must have had in mind when considering the ends of prayer just mentioned. It is universal, all-embracing. The prayer begins in adoration, with the use of the word 'hallowed'. The desire for God's Kingdom is pure petition. The request that God's will be done, is both a listening and a heeding to God so we might ascertain his will for us, as well as a petition 'for the whole state of Christ's Church here on earth'. When we ask to be given 'our daily bread' we are both petitioning God for our ongoing needs, but more importantly perhaps thanking him for granting them to us. The plea for forgiveness or propitiation speaks for itself and the desire to be helped in future to be delivered from the evil one is similar, and is in turn answered by the supplicant in the phrase 'for thine is the kingdom, the power and the glory' embodying that surge of faith alluded to by St Paul (Eph 6:11ff).

In the last hundred and fifty words the reader has the barest fragile outline of how I shall treat my subject over seven chapters, in order to provide a frame for each individual supplicant who may thereby be assisted to pray with true heart and a keen mind.

A slim book yet wide in wisdom and scholarly input which I would mention here is *The Lord's Prayer* by John Lowe, Dean of Christchurch at his death in 1960.[7] I refer to some of his interpretations and comments on the Lord's Prayer in the relevant chapters on each petition. He writes that 'nobody has exhausted its meaning, which is inexhaustible'. Nonetheless, this impressive and thoughtful scholar does not baulk in his attempts to analyse and compare the main gospel versions of the *Pater Noster*, as well as those who through the centuries have contributed to the great debate around vital aspects of the prayer.

He traces the earliest commentaries from Tertullian's treatise (circa 98-200 AD), through the Alexandrian and other Fathers of the early Church (such as Origen and St Clement), through St Gregory of Nyssa to St John Chrystostom, and St Augustine's sermons, to more contemporary writers such as Eckhart. Influenced to an extent by his own tutors, Lowe still pursues original and independent lines of thought. On balance I like his sympathy for the 'realised eschatology' (that is, the idea that the Kingdom preached by Christ has already come, though in a hidden way) school of Johannes Weiss and C. H. Dodd, of which I make mention in chapter 2 – Thy Kingdom Come.

For John Lowe, there is little doubt that the Lord's Prayer is centred around the belief that eschatology has already begun with the coming (and ministry) of Christ. Those sentiments belong to Pope John Paul II but they can be gleaned from our Redeemer himself, and in the prayer he taught his disciples.

I have earlier alluded to the help which Pope John Paul II gives in his writings and utterances to audiences all over the world, regarding the vitality of prayer. In conversation with the French religious writer, André Frossard, in the early 1980s, John Paul II said, 'the whole world has a right to expect much from the Pope so the Pope can never pray enough'. He stressed that in the priestly life the act par excellence of each day is the Holy Mass and that in order to reach this summit, 'which constitutes the perfect synthesis of prayer and the heart of our meeting with God in Christ', one must approach it through prayer.

Despite the liturgical nature of a priest's day, not only the Mass but also the Breviary, and together with all his other engagements, all activities, should be rooted in prayer as though in spiritual soil, the depth of which must never be too thin.

When Frossard ended this conversation, he did so in this significant way: 'Since prayer is the only significant weapon employed by Pope John Paul II, I asked one last question which summed up many others, and which was to receive the shortest answer in this dialogue. I asked him what his prayer for the whole world was, and he replied: "I call on mercy, yes, I call on mercy."'[8]

Speaking specifically about the Our Father from his residence outside Rome at Castel Gandolfo, in July, 1980, the Pope said that we remembered the prayer according to St Matthew's version.

Christ taught the words... the most perfect, the most complete; everything is contained in them. Christ's answer is not limited exclusively to the text, to the words we are to utter when we pray. It is a question of a far more pressing problem, and it could be said, also a far more complex one. 'We have to learn the Our Father.' If we can learn His reality in the full sense, then we have learned everything, and beyond all we have learned what absolute trust is. In that event, even when our prayers seem not to have been answered, in fact we will have learned that 'He never refuses you' for God has given us the substantial gift of the Holy Spirit, in consideration of his Son, and he gave his Son facing all the needs of the world, for the sins of the world. Neither is prayer selfish nor does it remain in isolation even when prayed in utter secrecy, since God is always present too. All prayer is thus outgoing and through its content, serves both the Church and the community.

In the context of the Pope's rather poignant and thus memorable words 'learning the Our Father' one is reminded of the whole mystery of the doctrine of the Trinity, and its interweaving between Father, Son and Holy Spirit.[8]

In turn I am reminded of the late President de Gaulle who consented to unveil a statue of our Lord in the precincts of a church in France. When the time came for the great man to perform the ceremony and the bishop asked what inscription the president cared to put at the base of the statue to mark the occasion, de Gaulle paused momentarily before answering in his perfect tongue, 'from the First Person of France to the Second Person of the Holy Trinity'.

In contrast though, whether with any greater humility I do not know, is the story of Archbishop Roberts, who when asked by a TV interviewer, 'Your Grace or Father? I believe you prefer to be called Father?' replied, 'Same as God, yes, Father.'

In my own life I have until now met only one cardinal

of the Church who sadly for the thousands who loved him, died two years ago. He was Owen, Cardinal McCann, a former Archbishop of Cape Town and up to his last days on earth, despite deteriorating health, a stalwart in love, sense and holiness. I do believe it was he who inspired me to pray with a greater devotion. We had met a few times but in crowds, corresponded a little, but only been alone on one occasion in his study in the Cathedral of St Mary. On that afternoon, fixing his wise old eyes upon me for a moment he enquired out of the blue, 'Do you pray often?' I told him that I did, and then he asked when and where. I told him when walking the dogs most often,⁹ which seemed to give him pleasure. 'Very good', he said, 'prayer is so important.' In fact I had come to see him with a view to writing a piece about the two great English Cardinals, Manning and Newman, whose centenary was imminent. But his digression intrigued me far more and prompted me to ask if I could do anything for him when on a visit to London the following week. 'Oh yes', came the reply 'would you please say a prayer for me in Westminster Cathedral?' I did so of course, on a pouring wet afternoon in November. It was the first time I had ever prayed there. At once there was the feeling of being spiritually at home and a knowledge that my humble mission was rewarded, and the prayer for His Eminence, my friend and God's servant, was graciously received.

There have obviously been myriad writers and commentators on the Lord's Prayer, so many of whom recognise its importance, yet others who mention it in passing, even some who dismiss it. The bibliography of the subject is thus so vast that it could itself be worthy of a book in itself. Allow me to mention some others at random of the very many I have read in preparation for this book. The unfortunate Bishop Latimer – burned at the stake in the reign of Queen Mary in 1555, – said of the *Pater Noster*: 'This prayer is the sum of all others.' *The Hastings Dictionary of the Bible* notes that a characteristic of the Lord's Prayer is its catholicity. It is already conscious of its worldwide destiny. Had it been merely a Jewish prayer of this date, it would certainly have been addressed to the Lord God of Israel (of our fathers) and would have contained a petition for the nation. In volume three it is stated a Christian's knowledge of its import grows with his spiritual experience'.[10]

The *Encyclopaedia Britannica*, under *Oratio Dominica* or *Pater Noster* tells us that the prayer lends itself to different interpretations amongst which are Existential or Eschatological.[11] The first interpretation would mean that the Our Father is rooted in the here and now of our existence; the second would mean that it looks forward to a time when God's plan is completed.[12]

The aforementioned work also points to the new Church of England translation of the prayer in 1977, drawing attention to such trivia as 'thy' becoming 'your' and 'as it is in heaven' becoming 'as in heaven'; 'this day' is excised in the request that our daily bread be given. 'Trespasses' become sins in the plea for forgiveness. 'Lead us not into temptation' however is changed to 'do not bring us to the day of trial'. I intend to make little comment on these changes in the English translation. It might seem to some that the hierarchy of that Church, presumably for the sake of greater simplicity or understanding has altered a faithful and beautiful translation of great renown, for no vital reason.

The distinguished author and masterful biographer, A.N. Wilson, in his historical biography *Jesus*[13] has a few provocative words to say about the Our Father; this in the midst of 256 pages of fascination and scholarship, spiced as it is with controversy. Indeed such an expert treatise is possibly spoilt for some Christians by its divisive and possibly contentious views. Unfortunately, so it seems to me, Mr Wilson does not make a serious attempt to discuss the Our Father. He notes that many New Testament scholars have questioned whether Jesus ever said these words (that is, the Lord's Prayer). But we are not forced to accept his conclusions.

The disciples ask Jesus 'teach us to pray' (Lk 11:1), they would have known that true prayer is rewarded though not always in the way we want. An example given is St Paul's suffering a thorn in the flesh (2 Cor 12:7-10), which he prayed to God three times might depart from him. But God had a higher reward for Paul, who had, after all, God's grace. Moreover Paul's weakness gave him humility and strength.

Another small book, which I came across by chance, entitled rather grandly, *The Catholic Religion*[14] was both excellent and concise so far as its section on the 'Our Father' went. Regarding the import of the prayer the author tells us that the prayer as its name implies was composed by our Lord, Jesus Christ, the best of all prayers and that which Christians should most frequently use being written in the gospels, used by apostles, martyrs and saints by the whole church in all countries and in all ages. It contains God's own statement of the needs of man, thus we have divine authority for believing all we ask is accord to the mind of God.

There are other works which have helped me gain a deeper understanding of the Lord's Prayer, dealing especially with the prayer's all-embracing value as a frame or skeleton on which to hang an agenda for our daily talk with God. I will acknowledge these within the chapters dealing with each petition.

The importance of prayer to American Catholics is well emphasised in a poll conducted in the mid 1970s, when the following question was put to the respondents (Religions of America): 'Which sources do you find most helpful when you are confused about what to believe as a Christian?' The answers, ranging from over 30% to 3% were illuminating. Prayer topped the poll at 31%; followed by Catholic friends (23%), priest (22%), spouse (21%), the Pope (4%) and Billy Graham (3%).

Mathematicians may query that the respondent's sources total 104% but the clerical duo of Pope Paul VI and Billy Graham may well account for this discrepancy! I find the sources an excellent and discerning mix. The result surely means that the majority of the respondents considered God not only the most important person to turn to and converse with, but also the most accessible. And if prayer is the most helpful antidote for a Christian's confusion, is it not equally the most powerful and practical way for a Christian to communicate regularly with the Holy Trinity. The Shepherd is ever ready to feed his sheep.

Much has been written about the time taken in praying. Estimates vary between five minutes a day to half an hour or more. Others (perhaps sensibly) have taken the view that since God is omnipresent as well as ever listening, it is helpful to pray more than once or twice in a day. In other words, not only when walking the dog or going to work by underground or bus, but possibly when walking in the street or jogging, as well as more traditionally, on our knees. As to the time given does it really matter? What to me is important is that I try in praying, to cover all the elements contained in that framework that Christ has given us; in other words that I include praise and love for God, and his love for us; that I follow what is his will for us on earth; that I thank him for our daily needs, for the gift of his sacraments and ask for their continuance in our hearts; that I petition for forgiveness and to be able to forgive; that God may prepare us for the life eternal; and that I conclude by having faith in his kingdom, his power and his glory. If our conversation along these lines lasts half an hour each day, then so be it. It is after all the best spent time there can ever be. But for some, more or less time may be equally wonderful and necessary. Life is seldom on an even keel, and either the petitioner or the Almighty may make their communion longer (or shorter) according to the need. It is such a personal matter, but worthy nonetheless of thought and planning. A discussion of importance with one's doctor, priest, union leader, boss, congressman or hospital matron, would prompt some preparation; how much more so with your God. But there is one immediate difference. With any of the earthly group an appointment would be required, whereas Our Father is always available.

Before leaving the subject of time for prayer, John Paul II has had some pithy things to say about it (Rome: 27 March 1980):

> Be men and women of prayer. The authentic Christian must be practising, that is he or she must live in the grace of God observing the commandments and carry out the Commandment of Charity concretely and continually. Only by a commitment of prayer is it possible to lead a life in grace and charity. The world is going through a crisis, also, because people do not pray, or pray little and badly.

There have been times when researching and writing this book, I have been afraid; afraid that anyone who presumes to examine and further to enlarge upon the prayer that Christ gave to his disciples and the world, is both arrogant and out of tune with the humility that Jesus also taught. When I first reacted to my own fears, it was because I feared to be presumptious. Then the second and I hope more considered reaction came – echoing our Lord's own words: 'Be not afraid', for Jesus will understand, nay applaud any of his people who love and believe in him, in order that they might, by their talents evangelize, provoke, draw out the salvation that he gave mankind. In other words if we believe he is the Son of God, the light, the truth, the way then no obstacle, no fear nor any ridicule can prevent us from spreading the redemption he has promised.

If in some way, great or small, this book helps the quality of prayer, the planning of it, and above all our nearness to God – Father, Son and Holy Spirit – that follows such a daily exercise; then the task of the author in writing it, and the reader who reads it will have been well worthwhile.

Cape Town, March 1997

1 Jn 17:24-26; see also chapter 1, p. 38ff of this book.
2 Tony Castle, *Through the Year with Pope John Paul II*, Hodder & Stoughton, London 1981. Reproduced by permission of Hodder and Stoughton Limited.
3 Some authorities (verse 14) emphasise here the role of the 2nd person of the Trinity by repeating the phrase and adding '...you shall ask *me* in my name...'
4 From *The Collected Works of St Teresa of Avila Volume One* translated by Kieran Kavanaugh and Otilio Rodriguez © 1976 by Washington Province of Discalced Carmelites ICS Publications 2131 Lincoln Road, N.E. Washington, D.C. 20002 USA.
5 Pope John Paul II, *Crossing the Threshold of Hope*, Jonathan Cape, London 1994.
6 Pope John Paul II, *Crossing the Threshold of Hope*, Jonathan Cape, London 1994.
7 cf J. Lowe, *The Lord's Prayer*, Clarendon Press, Oxford 1962.
8 A. Frossard, *Be Not Afraid*, Bodley Head, London 1984.
9 I had not then read St John Chrysostom's advice on when to pray, '...it is possible to offer fervent prayer... when walking in public... seated in your shop... even while cooking' (cf *CCC* 2743).
10 cf *Hastings Dictionary of the Bible*, Edinburgh 1902.
11 *Encyclopaedia Britannica.*, Encyclopaedia Britannica International Ltd, Sutton, Surrey (various years).
12 'It is the proper prayer of "the end-time"... the petitions [of the Lord's Prayer] ...rely on the mystery of salvation already accomplished ...in Christ crucified and risen.' (The *Catechism of the Catholic Church*, para 2771)
13 A. N. Wilson, *Jesus*, Sinclair-Stevenson, London 1992.
14 V. Stanley, *The Catholic Religion*, Mowbray & Co, London 1893.

CHAPTER 1

Our Father who art in Heaven, hallowed be thy name

The first petition contains the words 'hallowed be thy name', but before discussing these four words, permit me to do the same for the introductory words to the entire prayer, which preface each of the seven petitions in turn – the words 'Our Father who art in heaven'.

The word 'Our' is significant, since we are praying on behalf of all and not merely for ourselves.

St John Chrysostom says that Jesus is teaching us 'to make prayer in common for all our brethren. For He did not say 'my' father who art in Heaven, but 'our' father, offering petitions for the common body' (cf *CCC* 2825). Christ was telling his disciples that his father was also their father, and in turn he was to be considered the father of all who accepted him.

John Lowe in his work *The Lord's Prayer* suggests that the fatherhood of God is not a natural right, but a privilege conferred on the believer (cf Rom 8:15-23), although of course God is benevolent to all people, including sinners.

If this is so then it follows that when we pray the 'Our Father' in the way Jesus taught us, then from that moment on, if we continue to accept him, he is indeed Our Father.

When we call God 'Our Father', 'we ought to behave as sons of God, for now we have acquired an entirely new relationship with the Father (cf *CCC* 284); we have be-·come the people of God.

Thus at the very outset of the prayer Jesus was affecting an introduction to God the Father, to all believers, and at the same time was confessing and confirming that he was the Christ, the Son of God. There can be no mistaking the import of this introduction, since Jesus continues – 'who art in heaven'.

In other words the distinction between God and any earthly father was both swift and clear. In Aramaic the word *Abba* is used for father and this was the language Jesus mostly used.

Now, Abba would be the way a child addressed its father; a term of affection and endearment. But together with the possessive adjective 'our', he meant the disciples also to think of God as their father, as well as Christ's, in the sense that he is the universal creator and protector of all humankind.

Taking the introduction the inevitable further step, the twelve are in turn to teach their wider flock to petition God as 'Our Father'. From that time there is to be a unity in the brotherhood of Christ.

Looked at two thousand years later, the term 'Our Father' implies that however the Church has grown from St Peter's time, and whatever schisms there may have been or may be in the future, there is a universality in the words which will forever maintain the authority of Christ's prayer.

Now this invocation to God as Abba (or its Greek translation 'father') occurs through Jesus' lips one hundred and seventy times in the four gospels. This is of course highly relevant to Jesus' claim to be the Christ or Messiah sent by the Father. By his repeated reference to his Father, Our Lord stresses the interdependence between the First and Second Persons of the Trinity, which later would be coupled with the gift of the Third Person, in the Holy Spirit, to comfort and guide God's people after Father and Son are reunited in the heavenly Kingdom. Is there any doubt that these first two introductory words of Christ's prayer for the world provide a worthy title that will survive forever!

The relative clause 'who art in heaven' that follows is equally dramatic in that it confirms the Godhead from which Jesus was sent, as well as the eschatological nature of the prayer – from its outset. It also confirms the distinction from any earthly parent. Its real importance, when read together with the petitions that follow, is that the ultimate rule is not of this world, but the next. Furthermore it is a divine rule to which the Messiah will lead us if we follow him.

I have already hinted that the prayer to 'Our Father' in no way attempts to divide the Holy Trinity since the triune God is consubstantial and indivisible. It relates to the one God, who is recognised as Father, by those who through faith in his only Son are reborn of him by water and the Holy Spirit.

Finally, the 'Our' shows that God's love has no bounds and neither should our prayer. We pray for and with all, whether or not they know him. We pray for all creation.

Now follows the first petition. It is also the first of the three 'thy' petitions as they are sometimes called, distinguishing them from the remaining four 'us' petitions.

'Hallowed be thy name' should not be understood in a causative sense (since only God can make anything holy). Rather is it an invocation 'Thy name is holy'. It is recognising a fact. This is borne out in the Third Gospel which refers to: '...for the Mighty One...and holy is his name' (Lk 1:49).

Two of the Church Fathers refer to the petition thus – St Peter Chrysologus says, 'We ask then that just as the name of God is holy, so we may also obtain his holiness in our souls' (cf CCC 2814).

Tertullian says, 'When we say "Hallowed be thy name" we ask that it should be hallowed in us, who are in him (and by this) that we may obey the precept that obliges us to pray for everyone, even our enemies... we ask it shall be so in all men' (cf *CCC* 2814).

The first petition both praises God and confesses his divinity. We – his children – are at the same time asking to be allowed to emulate his holiness; that is insofar as our imperfection enables us, 'Be perfect, therefore, as your heavenly Father is perfect' (Mt 5:48).

In recognising that he is perfect love, we are drawn into the mystery of the Trinity as well as the whole drama of our pending salvation. By this I mean that even at this early stage of the prayer Jesus was foretelling his death and instilling in his disciples – thus to all believers – the need to know God fully.

For proof of the real eschatological meaning (I will explain this word a little more later, it has to do with the final destiny of things) we should go forward only a few years, to the prayer of the hour of Jesus:

> Father, the hour has come; glorify your Son so that the Son may glorify you, since you have given him authority over all people, to give eternal life to all whom you have given him. And this is eternal life, that they may know you, the only true God, and Jesus Christ whom you have sent (Jn 17:1-3).

Then right at the end of the same prayer, Jesus returns to this theme:

> Righteous Father, the world does not know you, but I know you; and these know that you have sent me. I made your name known to them, and I will make it known, so that the love with which you have loved me may be in them, and I in them (Jn 17:25-26).

Here then in the prayer of the hour of Jesus, as we have

called it, is confirmation that what Christ revealed in the first petition, was also revealing and unlocking the mystery of the resurrection, and the attainment of everlasting life. St Paul also recognises this unfolding drama in his letter to the Ephesians. In the course of this letter Paul says:

> ...he chose us in Christ... that we should be holy and blameless before him in love. He destined us for adoption as his children through Jesus Christ... in him we have redemption through his blood, the forgiveness of our trespasses, according to the riches of his grace (Eph 1:4-12).

Paul continues that God has made this known to us through Christ. Indeed the more one prays, researches and contemplates the petition (which has been my happy task) the clearer it becomes that within it is a signpost to Christ's redemptive plan as laid by his and Our Father.

Pope John Paul II, writing on the subject:

> The ultimate eschatological event was his redemptive death and his resurrection. This is the beginning of a new Heaven, and a new earth.[1]

The master-plan of man's salvation was afoot and part-revealed in the words 'Hallowed be thy name'.

In a more technical vein, the word 'hallowed' is of some interest. It comes from the Greek word *Hagiastheto* meaning make holy or honour and recognise as holy. Hence – 'all glory, laud and honour to thee Redeemer King...' in the Pascal hymn to the risen Christ; so the living, teaching Christ tells his followers to honour (the holiness of) the Father. Apart from the Greek word, the English verb to hallow means 'to honour as holy' from the Old English Halgian, or the Old High German, Heilagon.

Before leaving this analysis of the first petition, there are two general matters I feel it right to mention, and which I hope will be of interest and provoke thought.

The first of these concerns the gender of God the Father. Now there may be some who would question whether it is necessary to investigate this dilemma. I believe it is, in order to free ourselves from religious rancour over gender specific language. I am concerned at various changes or attempts to change gender specific language in the liturgies of the Churches. The concerns are genuine but I wonder if they are being pursued in a way that is entirely helpful. We might take the example at hand, where in the prayer we are discussing God is referred to as Father. Some might have us invoke God as 'Our Mother/Father' or even 'Our Parent'. But are not people who make such suggestions taking the word 'Father' too much at face value? I will limit myself to saying that we all might ask ourselves if we are falling into the trap of *Anthropomorphism*, the rather formidable Greek word that means attributing a human form and personality to God the Father. One immediately thinks of the artist, Michaelangelo, depicting God as a majestic old man with a white beard.

This danger of anthropomorphism is always with us. May I give one guideline: I find help – as so often – in the *Cathecism of the Catholic Church*. There, the writer states

> God transcends all creatures. We must therefore continually purify our language of everything that is limited, image-bound or imperfect, if we are not to confuse our image of God – 'the inexpressible, the incomprehensible, the invisible, the ungraspable' – with our human representations. Our human words always fall short of the mystery of God (*CCC* 42).

The second general matter I would care to discuss is of a quite different kind, and I imagine less contentious. I do not even say my thoughts are original in this matter, since the Lord's Prayer is so important, so pivotal and has enjoyed commentary, dissection and analysis by countless writers over two thousand years. True, the matter now to be raised, I have not heard discussed anywhere before; that does not mean no one else had thought about it. What now follows applies equally to the second petition as the first. In any event it is acknowledged in the third petition. I refer to the phrase added to that third petition – '…as it is in heaven'; the petition being of course – 'Thy will be done on earth'.

My point and my interest is that this phrase which comes after the third petition might well have been intended to cover all three of the 'thy' petitions. In other words, we could equally well say – 'Hallowed be thy name, as it is in heaven' and 'Thy Kingdom come as it is in heaven'. Does the phrase not make equal sense when fitted to petitions one and two? Purely as an exercise, and as we were taught in Law, let us reduce the problem *ad absurdum* by the following analogy.

May this tea be to our taste.
Let it also be strong.
And hot, as it comes from the pot.

Now take the common phrase, 'as it comes from the pot' and apply it to petitions one and two. It fits and makes sense in all three cases. If we were to add 'as it is in heaven' does it not add something to the first and second petitions? First: Your name is holy just as it is in Heaven. In other words: May we adore and confess you during our earthly lives, in the same way it is obvious you are supreme and holy in Heaven, as the King of Glory.

Does that invocation to the Father not become a heightened one; is it not lifted to an altogether higher plane?

I am not suggesting the phrase is in fact added each time; merely suggesting that we could properly add it in our hearts and minds when reciting the prayer, and maybe gain thereby.

Likewise, so as not to mention again in the next chapter; let us do the same exercise for the second petition.

We accept that your Kingdom has arrived here on earth, in the same way that we accept it has always been and is in Heaven.

43

In a similar way I will be suggesting in a later chapter that the *Doxology* at the end of the prayer fits and adds to both the sixth and seventh petitions. But that, as they say, is another story!

The Extended Prayers

1. Lord, help us daily to confess, and proclaim your divinity, as well as to emulate your holiness.

2. Our Father in Heaven, our Creator, and the ultimate reality, let us always adore you, and with your Son, our Lord Jesus Christ, who was made man, together with the Holy Spirit whom he sent in his place; may we show due reverence to your holy name and presence. Amen.

3. Let us love you more dearly and know you more nearly, as our lives ebb.

4. Teach us, Lord, always to do thy will, to work towards thy greater glory, and to use the talents you have so magnificently given us, to these ends; you who are our strength and our Redeemer.

5. Lord, hear our prayer and let our cry come unto thee.

6. When we pray to thee, let us praise thee, ask of thee and as importantly, listen to thy call to us so that in the silence of our communion we may be surrounded by the glory of creation, feel thy presence, and know what thou wouldst have us do. Amen.

7. Glory be to the Father, and to the Son, and to the Holy Spirit, as it was in the beginning, is now, and ever shall be; world without end. Amen.

Commentary on the Extended Prayers

Some of these seven prayers are well known, even if they are shortened versions, and others are original or hybrid. All, I hope are relevant to the message contained in the first petition. This message is both a statement of Faith as well as a petition of praise, and both elements are related.

1. There are three parts to this prayer:
   * confession or recognition of the divinity of God
   * to proclaim his divinity is second
   * emulation of his holiness is the third

We are asking first for God to help us know that he is divine, and since prayer to God is a two-way conversation, he is also asking us that question we may assume – in the same way he asked Peter, 'But who do you say that I am?

Our prayer to Him therefore is: 'You are the Messiah, the Son of the living God'.

You will recall Jesus' significant reply. Calling him by his name, Simon Barjona (son of Jona) he blessed him for 'flesh and blood hath not revealed unto thee, but my father which is in heaven' (Mt 16:15-17).

The second part – to proclaim his divinity – means telling God we wish to spread his Gospel and asking for help in fulfilling this duty. For the *Cathechism of the Catholic Church* say this about evangelization. The source of the words that follow is *Lumen Gentium*, the document drawn up at the Second Vatican Council in 1966.

> ...it is the right and duty of all lay faithful (in the Church) to work so that the Divine Message of Salvation should be known and accepted by all (*LG* 33; cf *CCC* 853).

The third part of the prayer asks God to help us imitate his holiness, for whilst we can never hope to be divine we can and should aspire to be holy.

Again we can never be perfect as he is, but we can strive towards a state of holiness in our daily lives, by asking to be morally and spiritually nearer to Christian ideals.

A number of Christians shy away from this aspiration, and I believe 'shy' may be the operative word. One might think perhaps it is lacking in humility to make this request. They are wary of being labelled 'holier than thou', and thought of as boastful prigs. But those who pray frequently and privately to God are nothing of the kind. I believe they can be entirely confident that the Triune God to whom they pray, will on the contrary bless them for their humility in asking for his grace.

2. This is a prayer in adoration of the Trinity. It addresses in one supplication the Three Persons, which is surely correct, since they are, or He is, one substance and cannot be divided, though the roles are separate at times, and of course historically they follow each other. After the Father, who is timeless, came the Son who was born man, and last the Spirit, known also as Counsellor, promised by the Son. As I will explain later I see the Spirit's coming as providing a second advent of the Son.

I put together this simple prayer, having read that the present Pope's predecessor, Paul VI was also known for his unashamed 'cult of adoration' for the Holy Trinity. Like some of the Fathers of the Church as well as popes, Paul VI believed in constant reverence and adoration of God the Father, Son and Spirit. This he encouraged by means of prayer, through the liturgy of the Church, including the beauty of music and the visible arts; by such artefacts as statues, shrines and crucifixes and especially in the personal devotion of Christian people: what they show to God in their daily lives, such as genuflexion and making the sign of the cross. Much lower down the scale, rather absurd niceties often appeal to me. Several spring to mind; perhaps I may mention two at random. When we leave a friend (and if we're really good, an enemy too) and say 'goodbye', would it not add something if we thought, only for a split second, what that used to mean? 'God be with you', has been contracted over the years to 'goodbye'. By thinking in this way we can love two beings (God and man) with one thought! That's an advance on killing two birds with one stone.

The second random thought relates, I think, to a more ancient custom; that of walking under a ladder. How often do we have the choice – whether to do so or walk around? There are dangers either way. In ancient times the ladder against the wall represented a mathematical equation, of 90°. If you chose to walk through the triangle you were breaking, and thus disrupting the Trinity. What would you do today? My answer is; it doesn't matter at all, so long as you think about it. Do you follow me? If you do think about your gyration, you'll be thinking about God! And in that way you will be loving him and communicating with him outside the normal times of prayer or worship.

However young or old we are, to know God more nearly, as the prayer asks we may, is surely worth striving for. But how? St Caesarea the Younger provides and answer. She is not a very well-known saint but I like what she says about the Gospels:

> There is no doctrine... more precious... than the text of the Gospel. Behold and maintain what our Lord and Master, Christ, has taught us by his words and accomplished by his deeds (cf *CCC* 59).

From these words one can infer that, one must not only know God – but make his acquaintance by study of the Scriptures – for God communicates himself in the Bible. Reading the Bible is thus a form of communion as the Eucharist is in a different way.

It follows then that if we can come to know Christ better through his life and teaching, we are also bound to love him the more dearly.

3. This is similar to the second prayer, but is aimed at those of us who are maturing, whether in age or wisdom or both. As we do so, might we come even closer to God in love, and might we also come to know him more nearly – in other words, more truthfully.

4. Teach us to do thy will. That's vital and should go without saying but it still needs to be said. Chapter 3 will go further into this. 'To work towards thy greater glory', the prayer continues, and to me it means this: during our normal day, and even when the day turns nasty and abnormal, we should make an effort in everything we do, to turn it towards God's glory, rather than our own.

The Jesuits have as their motto: ...*ad majorem gloria Dei* (to the greater glory of God). Let us pray that in small ways or in great, we may turn the events of our lives towards his glory. Whether it is waving and smiling and passing the time of day to a shop assistant, or one's boss; or in celebrating the birth of a child; let us momentarily at least, bring God into the event, and thank Him for his creation. There is a very sound maxim which says 'turn everything to your advantage' – even despair and defeat. There is always something to be gained and saved. How much more so can we apply this to him who created us, and will save us.

The final part of the prayer asks that we may make use of the talents that God has granted us.

Every single human being has God-given talents. Like genes they are legion and diverse. But, please, we plead to our Creator, let us exploit them 'to these ends' – towards furthering your will and exalting you, who made us for a purpose. Everyone of us, in his and her own direction, has something special to give. Enlighten us to give our best. The prayer ends by admitting that God is both our staff and our salvation.

5. This short exhortation is common in the liturgy of several Christian churches. I believe it needs to be said every now and again by those who pray. All right, it's superfluous, since of course He hears us. We don't have to remind him to listen! Nevertheless I find it a comfort, and if it's just nervousness, is there any shame in that? I suppose it's not so different from saying on the telephone, during a gap in the conversation, 'are you there?'

6. I believe I have already alluded to this prayer in the Introduction, when writing about the various types of prayer. Praise is certainly an important component. Petition is another. It is not only asking for ourselves and all humankind, but also – for example – asking for forgiveness, apart from material things. A third is the ability to listen as we pray. But that obviously does not mean going into a trance or expecting angels to appear and speak to us. They just might, and that would be a marvellous bonus, but we certainly should not expect it. That is why, more realistically, I suggest the silence of our listening may bring forth a sense of wonder and thankfulness at the glory of creation; of all we see and hear or feel around us, I ask that in this pause for reflection we might experience the beauty that God has created for us. In such reflective and thankful mood, may we experience the word or will of our Creator telling us what he would have us do for him. Almost always when I come to this part of my prayer, and pause to listen, I hear the same words, 'Be not afraid'. I then examine them.

7. This to me is an essential prayer, and I try and say it several times a day; but without fail every morning as soon as I awake.

NOTES

1   Pope John Paul II, *Crossing the Threshold of Hope*, Jonathan Cape, London 1994.

49

CHAPTER 2

Thy Kingdom come

Thus the second petition; simple and straightforward – or is it?

First we should note its position in the prayer, the second of seven. Now since the whole is dedicated to God the Father, Creator and First Person of the Trinity, it follows that the prayer would begin by introducing the Father, and revealing his relationship to Jesus.

The pride and importance of second place is given to the arrival of the Kingdom, and not the request that the Father's will be done as might perhaps have been expected. I say this because Christ had just announced his own divinity to his disciples; whether or not they realised it then is another matter. It would have been a natural progression to have gone on to ask that the Father's (as well as his own) commandments be obeyed. My Father is God in Heaven. We must do his will (by loving him and no other God, and by loving all his people). But no, that comes third.

The all important announcement of the Kingdom, following the introduction of God, seals the entire philosophy of the *Pater Noster*, which is that it is essentially an eschatological devotion. In my view this doctrine of eschatology is so vital to the full understanding of the Lord's Prayer, and particularly to the importance of the second petition, that I make no excuses for expanding on it now, as I promised earlier.

From the Greek word *Eschatos*, meaning last, plus the suffix 'logy', meaning a subject of study or of interest, or similarly a 'discourse' (cf Theo plus logy). Thus, we find in English the teaching about Heaven, about judgement, about the last things.

It has fascinated many minds, and my own is no exception. The all-pervading message of the first two petitions, and it also runs through the remainder, is of the last things. After all the Christian faith has two unique cornerstones: first that its founder is the Son of God who uniquely amongst all the great prophets and religious leaders, claims to be divine. The second unique cornerstone is that the Christian faith is based upon its redemptive foundation. Christ the Redeemer conquered the world by his death and resurrection. And these two fundamentals are reflected, in that order, in petitions one and two.

One scholar much concerned with the role of eschatology in the Bible was Johannes Weiss, in 1892, whose belief was that Jesus' Messianic self-consciousness gradually convinced him that it would be his own mission that would bring about the coming of the Kingdom of God in power.[1] This mission was confirmed by St Peter, who in turn was entrusted by Christ with the keys of the Kingdom. All this is recorded in St Matthew's Gospel, and I suggest that in the last verse of this chapter, Jesus goes further by telling his disciples:

...there are some standing here who will not taste death before they see the Son of Man coming in his kingdom (Mt 16:28).

Thus it can properly be said, the Kingdom has come with the resurrection. Hardly surprising then that the present distinguished incumbent of the throne of St Peter in a real but not definitive way has proclaimed:

Eschatology has already begun with the coming of Christ. The ultimate eschatological event was his redemptive death and his resurrection.[2]

But how do we know that the Kingdom had really begun with Christ's mission? What is the best evidence to suggest that during those three years around 30 AD, this was already happening? The answer is what Jesus Christ himself said and did at that time, and one of the clearest examples is recorded in St John's Gospel at chapter 11, and is well known to so many.

It concerns the death of Lazarus, the brother of Martha and Mary of Bethany. When Jesus visited the sisters, Lazarus had been dead and buried for four days. But he told Martha that her brother would rise again, to which she dutifully replied, 'I know that he will rise again in the resurrection on the last day'. To this came Jesus' hallowed and memorable comment, 'I am the resurrection and the life. Those who believe in me, even though they die, will live, and everyone who lives and believes in me will never die. Do you believe this?' Martha then confesses Jesus as the Christ, the Son of God (cf Jn 11:17-27).

As we know Jesus rewarded Martha's faith and that same day miraculously revived Lazarus, 'Unbind him, and let him go' (Jn 11:44).

C. H. Dodd, the English writer, born in 1884 and contemporary of Weiss, was the head of the school of 'Realised Eschatology'. By this I mean he takes the position that the Fourth Gospel portrays the End-time as having already arrived – been 'realised'. In other words that these times had already begun with Christ's advent and ended with his resurrection. Dodd dwells on this passage from the Fourth Gospel and compares it to earlier interpretations.

Dodd, ordained an Anglican in 1912 was a Fellow of

both Jesus College, Cambridge and University College, Oxford, as well as an Oxford New Testament Greek Professor, and holder of honorary degrees at both Yale and Harvard. Interestingly, he writes of the above passage, that it is typical of Johanine dialogue in that Martha is playing the usual part of an interlocutor with Jesus, which enables our Saviour to make the vital point – life is Christ's gift to mankind; in other words, Christ's gift to mankind is himself. The promise of eternal life may be enjoyed here and now by those who respond to the Word of God. Furthermore the same power which assures eternal life to all believers, will after the death of the body, raise the dead to renewed existence in a world beyond and this is also associated with judgement. Dodd summarises this when he say that knowledge of God which means Communion with him, through faith, in turn constitutes eternal life.[3]

He stresses the Greek word *Agapé* which he interprets as meaning a divine mutual indwelling (with God) and suggests that the true *Parousia* is found in the interchange of this *Agapé*, made possible through Christ's death and resurrection.

There are so many sources for the doctrine of realised eschatology. In his book, John Lowe contends the Kingdom of Heaven has come upon us, is at hand, has arrived. Heaven and earth are in this way brought together precisely because the heavenly one is the Father, exalted, but intimate and near through his redeeming Son.[4] Similarly Johannes Weiss views all the events of Jesus' life from such a perspective. We may note God's kingdom will come, since it has already begun – the double intent of the second petition. He writes: 'Thy Kingdom will come, since it has already begun'.

There are of course equally brilliant writers and thinkers who take an opposite view, including Albert Schweitzer, the Swiss scholar, philosopher and medical missionary. Schweitzer became a Doctor of Theology, but could not accept Christ's divinity. He claimed Jesus had no intention of founding a Church, nor did he look upon himself as being a Messiah. According to Schweitzer, he merely outlined the conditions for entry into the Kingdom in the very near future. He and others like him, thereby ignore Jesus' many statements of the presence of the Kingdom though we note with admiration that he spent most of his life as a medical missionary in Africa.

I mention again here C. H. Dodd. In his *Parables of the Kingdom*[5] Dodd says that there is a perfect fulfilment of the Messianic hope in Christ's earthly ministry. In imitating his obedience (to the Father) his followers can make the Kingdom for themselves and attain its (future) fruition.

In any event Christ had fulfilled Messianic hope, not only by his resurrection, but by his coming again at Pentecost through the Holy Spirit.

At the Last Supper he told the disciples he would next drink with them when he did so anew in his Father's Kingdom. And to the thief beside him on the Cross, he said, 'Today you will be with me in Paradise' (Lk 23:43).

At Vatican II – Dogmatic Constitution on the Church – it is stated the Church will be perfected only at the end of time (cf *LG* 48). This begins at the end of Christ's ministry and continues with the mission of the Holy Spirit in the Church.

Christ's disciples can be counted, I suggest, among the more than one thousand million Christians presently on earth, along with the faithful departed, those who will follow, as well as so many, who for a multitude of reasons have not or do not know Christ. Thus these disciples are only divided one from another because some are with him in glory, some are being purified, whilst others are still on earth or have yet to be created. But all are united in love, a bond not broken by death. From the first, man has been destined for the Beatific Vision and this is recorded in the Scriptures. But it is above all the Paschal mystery which is the central point of Christianity and the Christological approach to the last things.

Returning to the text of the second petition 'Thy Kingdom Come' and treating the words eschatologically, appertaining to the 'last things', it is surely a fair interpretation that God's Kingdom had come, in the sense that when Jesus taught the words, nothing would ever be the same again! The Son of God had revealed himself, a new reign had plainly begun and very soon was to expand and come even further to fruition with the arrival of the Holy Spirit. One cruciual example of the furtherance of the Kingdom is seen in the role of the Papacy in the Church's history.

It was the third time Jesus showed himself to the disciples since the resurrection, and Peter, upset by the Master's persistent questioning told him, 'Lord you know everything (so) you know that I love you.' We all know the response to that from Jesus; the command: 'Feed my sheep' (Jn 21:17).

Thus Christ founds his Church on Peter, the Rock. (Both words have the same meaning in Greek; the word is *Petra*.)

From then on, obedience to Peter and his successors has found a special place in God's plan of salvation, for this Church has become the mystical Body of Christ. My point is that from then on 'these keys of the Kingdom' that were handed down meant that the risen body of Christ lived on in his Church, which also becomes the 'Temple of the Holy Spirit'. And once again there is continued fusion between the Second and Third Persons of the Trinity, just as between the First and Second. In other words, the Kingdom has not only arrived; its future on earth is continuing and is assured in its succession.

The keys were entrusted to all God's people on earth through Holy Church, in universal succession, by Christ's vicars or agents, '...whatever you bind on earth will be bound in Heaven...' (Mt 16:19).

How does this succession work, and can it really be said to be a continuing tradition and a furtherance of the Kingdom?

No Pope is perfect, just as no man is without sin, but

they are to reflect and oversee the authority of the Church which was Christ's creation. The Bible and particularly the New Testament is the main authority for the Church, but it is through the Tradition of the Church and its teaching that Scripture is constantly interpreted. Hence Christ's teachings are not exhausted by the gospels. Indeed if we read the last verse of the Fourth and last Gospel in its final chapter the writer tells there were so many other things which Jesus did – and which have never been recorded – since the world itself could not contain the books that would be written.

How this Tradition of the Church – as defined at the First Vatican Council in 1870, is to be reconciled with differing opinions expressed on matters of dogma and liturgy was not settled. But the infallibility of the pope does provide Church with a living tradition, and Pope Pius XII is on record in 1950 (*Humanae Generis*) as saying, 'Together with the sacred sources of scripture and tradition God has given a living *Magisterium* to his Church...'. And the office of the Pope forms part of this Magisterium.

It took 80 years from Vatican I for the Pope to put the dogma of papal infallibility into action for the first time in 1950, when he proclaimed the Assumption of the Blessed Virgin Mary.

As Jaroslav Pelikan concludes in his masterful chapter on these matters – and I feel obliged to quote it in full:

The mature Roman Catholic has similarly learned how frail even the noblest of men can be, but he has also learned how the power of God can manifest itself in the very midst of this frailty and sin. Peter denied his Lord. Yet into Peter's apostolic hands Christ put the keys of the Kingdom; to him Christ gave the command to 'feed my sheep'; on this rock Christ has built his Church. Despite the weakness of men, including Peter, the gates of Hell have *not* prevailed against it.[6]

Two thousand years after Peter, this same obedience to Christ continues unabated. That is the message.

When Jesus appointed the Seventy, in pairs and as lambs among wolves, he instructed them to tell all who would listen and even those who wouldn't, that the Kingdom of God is come near you. Here again he was speaking eschatologically, knowing what was to happen to him. It was then he told these evangelizers of the faith, that they that hear you, hear me... He went further of course, and with utter logic as one would expect. It stands to reason, 'those who despise (or dismiss?) me, also despise you' (cf Jn 15:18) I hate the idea of our Lord being despised, even though it is bound to happen, but looked at from the other side of the coin, how uplifting and rewarding if you and I, as evangelizers, can communicate something of his teaching, and reach a receptive audience. What does this mean? It means that God's people can influence waverers, but much more importantly, can 'be heard by God'. That surely must be the ultimate joy in a believer's ear. Through our effort, which is no more than our duty, someone somewhere has received the Word of God; and He has thus responded to her, and just maybe, as a result, that person is assured of everlasting life in the Kingdom of Heaven.

When we pray 'Thy Kingdom come' we are asking that God's *basileia*, his divine reign or dominion, will be extended here and now – *elathò* – to the hearts of individuals and in the world as a whole. In other words the Kingdom is to be with us in our own time.

St Mark tells us, 'Jesus came to Galilee proclaiming the good news of God, and saying, 'The time is fulfilled, and the Kingdom of God has come near; repent, and believe in the good news' (Mk 1:14).

Likewise St Luke records Jesus' answer to the Pharisees as to when the Kingdom would come. Not, he told them, with observation. Neither should they say, 'Look, here it is! or 'There it is!' For, in fact, the Kingdom of God is among you.' Not will be, but *is* (cf Lk 17:20).

The most wonderful example of this must be the Sacrament of the Eucharist, when the Kingdom is truly in our midst.

St Paul writes to the Church at Corinth saying that God, through Christ, has given us a guarantee in the Spirit (2 Cor 1:22).

St Cyprian said it may even be, 'The Kingdom means Christ himself, for he is our resurrection... in him we rise... in him we shall reign' (cf *CCC* 2816).

When we pray this petition we know that Christ's gift to us and his promise of redemption, is Christ himself.

From his advent, through his ministry, at his death and resurrection; at his coming before his ascension, and likewise by the coming of his Holy Spirit, has this Kingdom really been initiated. We pray for it to be fulfilled in us, so that at death we too may have eternal life. Thy Kingdom come.

Let me conclude my analysis of the second petition on a lighter note, but for a reason since, amusing moments often allow the mind to reflect on deeper things. In the 1950s I was a twenty-year-old supporter of the Labour Party in London. Nye Bevan, the then Minister of Health in Attlee's Labour Government, and one of Parliament's greater orators, came to speak at an election meeting in Fulham, and in the course of a speech before a rowdy audience equally divided in its loyalties, a man rose to his feet and shouted above the din, 'Behold the Kingdom of Bevan is nigh!' He was clearly familiar with Mark's Gospel, as were most of the audience, who were hugely amused by the analogy. Bevan's earthly kingdom never came to pass, although he had achieved considerable political power. In stark contrast Jesus was never a political leader and refused to become one. Hence when he taught his disciples to pray for the Kingdom that had come, it was far from being a political, let alone a subversive prayer. He had already spurned the temptation of ruling over 'the kingdoms of the world'. Jesus Christ made it abundantly clear that he was not of this world, other than to be sent into it briefly, in order to save it from sin, and bring its people, his people, to the Kingdom that he brought to earth from Heaven.

Whoever thought this chapter on the coming of the Kingdom would be short and to the point, I fear they were very wrong about the shortness, but please God it is to the point! I have been helped, and inspired also, by researching the petition, but the hope is to fire my readers as well, which after all is the joy of evangelization. However it should not be selfish, but in order to share.

May I therefore conclude by returning briefly to C.H. Dodd, the writer of an important (if at times debatable) commentary on St John's Gospel. He writes with particular regard to the Evangelist's understanding of Christ's divine mission – that of bringing Christians to everlasting life.

Dodd finds 'particularly illuminating', these words of St John:

> No one has greater love than this, to lay down one's life for one's friends. You are my friends if you do what I command you. I do not call you servants any longer, because the servant does not know what the master is doing; but I have called you friends, because I have made known to you everything that I have heard from my Father. You did not choose me but I chose you. And I appointed you to go and bear fruit, fruit that will last, so that the Father will give you whatever you ask him in my name. I am giving you these commands so that you may love one another (Jn 15:13-13).

On these verses Dodd comments that they are sealed by (Christ's) supreme act of *Agapé*. He goes on to say that Christ is actually here imparting eternal life to them, that is to say, his disciples. But we know, if we believe, that we too are his disciples.

The Extended Prayers

1. We believe that through your death and resurrection you have opened the Kingdom of God to all believers.
2. That the Kingdom of Heaven which is eternal life is ours by your redemptive grace, to all who have knowledge of you, Father, Son and Holy Spirit and keep your Word.
3. St Paul has told us that the Kingdom of God is righteousness and peace and joy in the Holy Spirit (Rom 14:17). Let us therefore serve Christ in these things, that we may fulfil the Kingdom.
4. May we be sanctified by the truth of the Father as imparted to the Son, and by him to us; that we all be one. In this way, Lord may we find our divine indwelling with you.
5. Lord we believe that your words are the light and the way to your father's Kingdom. Give us the strength to receive your light and follow your way, which are our strength and our Redeemer.
6. St Peter confessed: 'You are the Messiah, the Son of the living God' and you Lord Jesus, told him 'and on this rock I will build my Church...' (cf Mt 16:16-18). We believe that at Pentecost and the foundation of your Church by the Holy Spirit, was established a unique place on earth for the Kingdom of God. May the Holy Spirit – working through the vicars of Christ and all your apostles – give us the Catholicity and universality we must follow. By this tradition, dogma and liturgy may we be fulfilled in thy Kingdom, which has now come and has no end.

Analysis of the Extended Prayers

I have set down six prayers to be said after praying the petition 'Thy Kingdom Come'. As will be seen these prayers summarise much of the commentary earlier in the chapter. I would hope that they assist in concentrating our minds on the eschatological meaning of the petition as well as giving some fullness and beauty to the bare bones.

The first five form a single group of prayers, which mainly reflect pertinent passages from the gospels, whilst the sixth is a composite prayer summarising the effect of Pentecost on the Kingdom.

On a daily basis the supplicant may find it helpful to pray any one or more of the first five plus the sixth.

1. This in a nutshell emphasises what Jesus told Martha upon raising Lazarus from the dead. 'I am the resurrection and the life' (Jn 11:25); and 'Now is the judgement of this world' (Jn 12:31). By his advents (sic) Christ came to save mankind which he fulfilled by his death and resurrection. Thus he opened the kingdom to all who believe in him.

2. This prayer makes three points. First the Kingdom is eternal life; it is not transitory like our life on earth. Secondly it is a gift from God the Father, who sent his only Son to die for our salvation, and after his resurrection gave us the Spirit of truth to guide us to the same. Thirdly in return for this redemption we should believe in (know) the consubstantiality of the Trinity and keep God's commandment of love.

3. Note that St Paul, apostle of Jesus, in his letter to the Romans tells us how the Kingdom *is*, in the present tense, and thus within and around us. It is the righteousness of Christ's ministry on earth, the peace of God which passes all understanding, and the joy of his Holy Spirit, which through his Church here on earth, teaches and inspires us. In order to bring this Kingdom to its fulfilment in us, we should understand these things, and in so doing serve God who loves us.

In order to fulfil the Kingdom, we God's people, must understand that the kingdom has come to us.

St Paul, whose earliest writing was perhaps as little as

just over twenty years after the resurrection, knew and does his level best to impart this knowledge in us if we will only find and accept it. Paul, if it was him (and many reputable scholars are certain it wasn't) reminds his Hebrew congregation that 'Christ did not enter a sanctuary made by human hands... but he entered into Heaven itself... on our behalf' and not for an annual sacrifice, as the High Priest but, 'once and for all *at the end of the age* to put away sin by the sacrifice of himself'. And just as it is appointed for men to die once, and after that comes judgement, so Christ... will appear 'a second time, not to deal with sin but to save those who are eagerly waiting for him' (Heb 9:24-28).

Paul also told the Corinthians the same thing: '...Then comes the end, when he hands over the kingdom to God the Father...' (1 Cor 15:24-26).

Likewise the Romans: 'For the Kingdom of God is not food and drink but righteousness and peace and joy in the Holy Spirit' (Rom 14:17).

And the Ephesians: 'But God who is rich in mercy... even when we were dead through our trespasses, made us alive together with Christ – by grace you have been saved – and raised us up with him and seated us with him in the heavenly places in Christ Jesus' (Eph 2:4-6).

There are many references in the Fourth Gospel to God's judgement of humankind. What might we expect and when? Chapter 8 is to me a veritable fount of truth in this regard, dealing as it does with Jesus' words both to Pharisees and Jews, who found it difficult to understand who he was. When they deny him, Jesus assures the Pharisees that he is telling them the truth about himself and his divinity as the Son of God: 'Whoever follows me will never walk in darkness but will have the light of life' (Jn 8:12).

He even goes so far as to say to them that, as in Pharisaic law, he can prove his divinity, by the corroborating evidence of God his father.[7]

In the same way: 'Yet even if I do judge, my judgment

is valid; for it is not I alone who judge, but I and the Father who sent me...' and later: 'and the one who sent me is with me; he has not left me alone...' (Jn 8:29).

Are these two sayings in themselves not sufficient proof of the union of Father and Son? Can there be any possible doubt that Christ Jesus is part of God as well as being his Son, who was 'made man' by the Father.

To the Jews who believed in him, he told them they were truly his disciples and 'the truth will make you free' (Jn 8:31-2).

When they continued to argue with him and failed to understand, Jesus put it this way: 'I do not seek my own glory; there is one who seeks it and he is the judge. Very truly, I tell you... whoever keeps my word will never see death' (Jn 8:50-51).

Does this not mean that judgement is already dispensed with once a commitment is made to Christ?

This earth-shattering maxim – for that is what it is for me – is repeated in similar form in chapter 12 of St John's Gospel (Jn 12:44-50) and never to my mind more clearly than by the crowd that heard Christ say 'now is the judgement of this world...' (Jn 12,31).

In other words there is a limitation of judgement, which will become the concern of the wicked; God's role being to bring sinners to repentance.

Again in chapter 16 Jesus tells the disciples: '... it is to your advantage that I go away; for if I do not go away, the Advocate will not come to you; but if I go, I will send him to you... and when he comes, he will prove the world wrong about sin and righteousness and judgement' (Jn 16:7).

The Kingdom has already arrived with Christ's ministry on earth. The second petition invokes the beginning of the end times, which themselves will end with the resurrection and the conquest of death. Furthermore it is the evil of this world that will be judged and its perpetrator, the 'anti-Christ' – not those who see the light and follow it.

4. The fourth extended prayer is plucked from the illuminating and beautiful prayer of the hour of Jesus, as recorded by St John, when Christ prayed to his Father on behalf of all humankind.

If the Lord's Prayer taught by Christ is the foundation of all prayer and the key to our communion with God, then how much more is this prayer of Jesus to his Father, the symbol of and the key to the unity of God with man. Its repetition is extraordinary, making the desire so powerful for the complete communion between Father, Son and children.

Jesus is asking God to make us holy through his truth, as imparted by Christ to ourselves, in order that we might all be *ad idem*. In this way we cannot but be part of the kingdom.[8] In this way we cannot fail to find our 'divine indwelling' *Agapé* in Heaven, which is the life eternal, and in glory.

5. The fifth extended prayer: St John's Gospel has many references to Jesus using the analogy of light, meaning truth. Those who do not use this gift of light will stumble in darkness. His disciple, St Thomas, asks how we shall find where he has gone, and is told by his master, 'I am the Way'. We recognise these things and as therefore for strength – when the flesh or the spirit is weak – to receive his truth and follow his path. The latter also means we are bound to evangelize by leading others along his way, and that includes those we love and also our enemies. It is our duty for we know the route as well as the vital fact that it leads to the kingdom, which is come.

6. The final prayer relates to the effect of Pentecost on the fulfilment of the Kingdom. It invokes St Peter's confession which leads to Jesus telling him that he will be the rock on which the Church will be founded. We believe that the foundation of Church at Pentecost establishes a bridge to the Kingdom; that the Holy Spirit working through the Vicars of Christ, as well as by the tradition,

dogmas and liturgy of Church, will assist us to follow and fulfil in us his Kingdom that has no end.

This second coming is both momentous and dramatic. Consider the words of St Basil: 'Through the Holy Spirit we are restored to Paradise, led back to the Kingdom of Heaven and adopted as children, given confidence to call God Father and to share in Christ's grace, called children of light and given a share in eternal glory' (cf *CCC* 736).

For some 2,000 years, starting with St Paul and the other apostles following Christ, there has been an out-pouring of the Word of God.

Following the gospels, epistles and the Acts of the Apostles, came the Fathers of the Church and all the saints throughout the ages. To these, eminent theologians have added their wisdom and learning. Thus are we taught to pray such simple utterances of faith as the early prayer: 'Lord Jesus Christ, Son of God, have mercy on us sinners' (cf Mk 10:47, Lk 18:13), or the equally ancient and evocative 'Come Holy Spirit, fill the hearts of your faithful and enkindle in them the power of your love.'[9]

The whole liturgy of the Church which is constantly added to, assists in our devotion to and love of God, through the Holy Spirit.

Finally the extended prayer evokes the continuity, through the apostolic succession, by the Vicars of Christ and the tradition given by the Church's various constitutions.

Thus the prayer seeks to dispel the idea that dogma and doctrine are dull appendages, to be scorned as meaningless inventions of man. To my mind such a notion is blown away by the modernity of its thought as well as the in-spired discipline which emanates from Christ's universal Church. This Church is the body of which he is the head.

From one who contributed much to the Church he converted to, John Henry Newman has this to say: 'Dogma has been the fundamental principle of my religion (for) religion as a mere sentiment is to me a mockery.'

The once Anglican Archdeacon of Chichester became a Cardinal of the Roman Catholic Church.

The more I consider it the more I realise and commend the sense of Cardinal Newman's intellect all those years ago. For dogma should not be narrow nor become stale or out of date. It is to me the very essence of the Church's teaching, in the way it reveals divine truth. These are hallowed words enshrined in papal and conciliar declarations.

Just as God's Kingdom has, we pray, arrived in our hearts and minds so does his Church on earth have the ongoing duty, through the apostolic succession to teach and govern the people of God. To this great end the dogma and the doctrine that church propounds is far from static, and must develop with care and in truth.

NOTES

1   cf J. Weiss (ed. & trans. F. Grant), *The History of Primitive Christianity*, Macmillan & Co, London 1937.
2   Pope John Paul II, *Crossing the Threshold of Hope*, Jonathan Cape, London 1994.
3   C. H. Dodd, *The Interpretation of the Fourth Gospel*, Cambridge University Press, Cambridge 1953.
4   J. Lowe, *The Lord's Prayer*, Clarendon Press, Oxford 1962.
5   C. H. Dodd, *Parables of the Kingdom*, Charles Scribner's Sons, New York, 1961.
6   J. Pelikan, *The Riddle of Roman Catholicism*, Hodder & Stoughton, London 1960.
7   By means of a second witness to the truth; also demanded by the law.
8   'When I am lifted up I will draw all men to myself' (Jn 12,32), says the *Catechism of the Catholic Church* – by his death (Christ) *would accomplish the coming of his kingdom*, (*CCC* 542)
9   Roman Missal, Pentecost.

CHAPTER 3

Thy will be done on earth as it is in Heaven

The third petition: Thy will be done

The burden of this petition, which may be called the petition of love is that God desires that all men be saved and come to the knowledge of the truth.

To this end his son, Jesus Christ, gave us 'a new commandment, that you love one another. Just as I have loved you, you also should love one another' (Jn 13:34).

We may say that this commandment summarises all the others, expressing his entire will.

St Luke's Gospel records the commandment of love by giving us our Lord's words to the lawyer who asked him what he should do to inherit eternal life. Jesus first asked the lawyer what was for him an easy question to answer: 'What is written in the Law...?' The lawyer answered, 'You shall love the Lord your God with all your heart... soul and strength, and with all your mind; and your neighbour as yourself' (Lk 10:25-28 and cf Mt 22:37-40).

In *Gaudium et Spes* (*GS* 24,3) we read that man can be sure that God wants him to love truly; and he can be sure that God will not refuse him his grace; that he desires his salvation.

In similar vein the early theologian, Origen, says that if we commit ourselves to Christ we can become one with him and thereby accomplish his will in such a way that it will be perfect on earth as it is in Heaven (cf *CCC* 2825).

St John puts it this way: 'We know that God does not listen to sinners, but he does listen to one who worships him and obeys his will' (Jn 9:31).

Bearing this last in mind, could there be a greater reason than this for praying the Lord's Prayer?

Whilst therefore the single commandment of Love is what God asks of us, and what we here petition him that we might fulfil; the command is twofold. We must love God and all mankind. Moreover there is only one God – God the Father – who gave us his only Son who sent us the Holy Spirit.

We should remember too 'thy will' is God's will. St John's Gospel uses Jesus' words: 'I have come down from Heaven not to do my own will, but the will of Him who sent me' (Jn 6:38).

The third petition is rich in the persual of duty and the reaping of reward. We are to pray that God's will be done. We are to 'go out and teach all nations' as Christ commanded. Jesus' disciples were to carry out that duty, and in turn through the ages every man and woman has that same duty, but the reward is great. St Matthew ends his gospel telling us just how great, with Christ's own words ringing in his reader's ears. He is telling the world for evermore that if they do his will then, '… I am with you always, to the end of the age. Amen' (cf Mt 28:19-20).

We are to do the will of the father in Heaven which is perfection. Of course this can only be done with imperfection and in humility, but we are to outreach ourselves in an effort to achieve perfection. Perhaps it follows that such outreaching cannot be by our own achievements alone, but if the effort and the faith are present then God's grace will tip the scales.

St John Chrysostom tells us that our prayer must be universal – for the whole world – for Christ's prayer teaches:

'thy will be done on earth, the whole earth, so that error may be banished from it, truth take root in it, all vice be destroyed on it, virtue flourish on it, and earth no longer differ from heaven' (cf *CCC* 2825).

It is easy to neglect the last five words of this petition, not because they are in any way superfluous, but in the sense that they are a kind of *doxology* or liturgical Gloria. In my view they are not to be neglected.

The words 'as it is in heaven' are reinforcement to the others. They assert boldly and in faith the vital premise that God's will is supreme in his Kingdom. Those who live forever in Heaven are enlightened by the glory of God. There, his will, the love of God and the people of God who dwell in him, is absolute and perfect. Looking backward then from that height of perfection, we are bidden to pray and work (*ora et labora*) for this commandment of love to be perfected in our and all other lives on earth.

Let St Augustine enrich us with his interpretation of these words in his Sermons.

> It would not be inconsistent with the truth to understand the words: "Thy will be done on earth as it is in Heaven" to mean: in the Church as in our Lord Jesus Christ, himself; or in the bride who has been betrothed, just as in the bridegroom who has accomplished the will of the Father... (cf *CCC* 2827).

But there is something else about these final words in the petition on God's Will, which in my view makes them of great importance. I would deal with the choice we have between disillusionment or the 'triumph'. Let me explain it this way. Discussion about the divinity of God, the very existence of Christ as the Son of God, as well as the veracity of the New Testament, has never been greater than now, as we approach the end of the second millennium since his crucifixion. A welter of books has recently been published, media coverage of all kinds and a great debate rages around the major tenets of our faith. It seems moreover – and this to a degree should be healthy – that people's appetite for such debate is both voracious and unsatisfied. Those who question the Christian faith in this way do not in the main emanate from adherents of other religions. No. Those who question the Christian faith thus I see as the atheists, even some agnostics. More often than not they are painstakingly clever and assiduous in their historical and biblical research. Of course some of them determined to attack Christian beliefs whenever possible and to the greatest effect.

We know that Christians have a duty to 'always be ready to make your defence to anyone who demands from you an account of the hope that is in you' and thus to defend our belief against unjust criticism; and we know that we are to do it 'with gentleness and reverence' (1 Pet 3:15-16).

The recurring message is usually that Jesus Christ existed merely as a man, was in no way the Son of God, and when he claimed to be, was therefore fraudulent. He wrought no miracles, did not rise from the dead, nor reappeared as stated. Moreover, he was a propagandist for a new order, which was anti-Roman colonialist, pro the Cynical Sect, and so on. But Jesus asked that God's will be don, as it is in Heaven.

There are even modern scholars* who will support the notion that the Lord's Prayer is probably authentic, as it is recorded in the New Testament. If this be right, then we must thank God for such scholars since the *Pater Noster* is the epicentre of all prayer, and as I see it, the inspiration for all Christ's teaching.

Unfortunatley some scholars have denied the 'historical' authenticity of many of Jesus' sayings. I think it is fair to question the solidity of the grounds for His denials. Furthermore, and perhaps more significantly, we can ask if they have failed to realise the power of these words in themselves – particularly those of the Lord's Prayer.

But let me then return to the words '…as it is in heaven'. Are these the words of a revolutionary leader or a cynic? Do they convey to you a desire to implant a new order on earth in defiance of Caesar? Would they suggest an attempt to proffer a political programme of reform contrary to that existing under the Jews or their Roman masters?

In other words Jesus' instruction to his disciples to pray for God's will to be done on earth, and which he later elaborated to mean that love of God and for mankind should supersede all (including let us never forget, love for one's enemies – political and social), could never be interpreted as usurping the Jews, or the Roman Empire, nor any others in the then-known world.

And coupled with the words, the provision, 'as it is in heaven' it becomes doubly improper to suggest otherwise.

If, just if, Jesus had ended his petition without these five words, then at a gigantic stretch of the imagination it could be suggested that revolution was afoot; that the superimposition of God's will upon man's was imminent. All this notwithstanding it was made clear, the only thing at stake was love.

But when one adds as a yardstick, that what this means is measured by the joy and peace, the tranquillity and love of Heaven – does it not prevent any attempt to portray Christ as anything but the Prince of Peace?

The Extended Prayer

By our baptism into Church you have made us disciples to do your will on earth, and to work always for your greater glory.

In humility yet with joy may we strive to do just that, which also means that we should teach all men (even as your first disciples did) to believe and do your will.

In so doing let us overreach all boundaries of our minds and bodies, remembering that this earth in which we live may not be the home of all your flock, and that in other universes there could be countless others who know or do not know you.

We thank you, Lord, for giving us free will in all things. Help us to use it well, and still to do your will.

What is your will, dear Lord?

There are two commandments; the first that thou shalt love the Lord thy God with all thy heart and voice and strength, and love no other God but thee (Mk 12:30; Lk 10:27).

Let us also pray for all those who 'know not the name of the Lord Jesus'; and for those who are Muslims, Buddhists, Jews or of other faiths or none; for agnostics and atheists and for those who have lost you along the way.

Hear our prayer, O Lord, and let our cry come unto thee.

The second commandment is like unto the first. Thou shalt love thy neighbour as thyself. On these two commandments hang all the law and the prophets.

Regarding the second commandment of love, let us pray for all God's people, whether near and dear to us or not and also for our enemies including X, Y and Z.

May we love and forgive them and try to find understanding for their hatred/avoidance/malice towards us or those we love. We ask you also to forgive them. Let us and them practise the reciprocity of forgiveness. Where reconciliation is possible, Lord, bring it. Let us at the same time be not afraid and hold fast to that which is true and right and of good Christian report. Never allow us to dispense with these values, in an effort to appease, nor to avoid humiliation from others.

Let us now remember and pray for all who are close to us and known to us.

For my darling wife, V – Lord, give her love and faith in thee, and bring her at length to everlasting life. Endow her with health and safety and protect her this day from evil. We bless and thank you Lord, for the blessed sacrament of Marriage that you have given us together with the other sacraments. May this *mysterion* prepare us for the life eternal. We thank you for Christ's ministry on earth and his first miracle wrought in Cana where, with his mother present, at the marriage feast he turned water into water and wine, and blessed by his being there the state of marriage, which state tells us of Christ's love for his bride, the Church. So let it be for us, with the priest to bless and witness the sacrament between the bride and groom; that we might strive to live our lives in communion with Christ – so that we might be one with him, and each other.

For our beloved children (named, with any spouses and children), keep them safely in your care this day and protect them from all evil. Give them faith, O Lord, in thee.

For our parents we call forth thy blessing. Protect them in frailty and age. We thank them for our upbringing and their love for us. May we always honour them.

We pray for all the saints in Heaven, for the souls of the faithful departed (including our parents, grandparents, loved ones) that you will grant them even more enlightenment and joy.

May these souls be interceded for especially by those religious, who by their grace will pray for them through their divine vocation.

(Pray here for any by name who have recently died.)

O Lord might thy mercy extend also to those souls still being purified. We pray for all who have not yet arrived in thy Kingdom, and ask thy compassion for them.

Likewise, we pray for all those who may be beyond redemption in our limited understanding; nevertheless praying for our Saviour's love for all sinners.

We pray for all deacons, priests, bishops in thy Church including Fr M... etc, the Holy Father and all religious, who pray continually for us and all the world.

Lord bless our godparents P and Q and our godchildren R, S, T (mentioning one each day).

Let us pray for all those awaiting trial, surgery, death (or any other adversity), and all who work for them.

We ask you, Lord, to bless this day all those who are weak, hungry, lonely, lost, in danger, poor, and all nonhuman creatures great and small. Give them succour, hope and thine abounding love.

For all who are strong, rich, powerful, help them to have humility and to realise their special responsibilities to all mankind.

We pray for peace throughout the world for consensus rather than confrontation, love over hate, faith over despair. Let us pray, sweet Jesus, for the attainment of thy Kingdom, and for the whole state of Christ's Church here on earth. Amen.

Commentary on the Extended Prayer

Modern Christianity, just as 2000 years ago in the early Church, is all about the ministry of evangelization and the Gospel of Christ. That is why in the extended prayer to the third petition I begin by acknowledging a fundamental dogma: that by our baptism and membership of the Church we automatically become disciples of Christ. And I am not supposing that the reader is ordained or a religious, but a clerk who is not in Holy Orders, a bus conductor or a surgeon. But whoever she or he is, this discipleship carries with it both a right and a duty to propagate his Gospel, and to do his will.

Remember what St Paul said: 'Woe to me if I do not proclaim the gospel' (1 Cor 9:16).

The Holy Father tells us that the Church takes up anew each day a struggle that is a struggle for the world's soul... the encyclical *Redemptoris Missio* speaks of modern Areopagi... as the worlds of science, culture and media the worlds of writers and artists, the worlds where the intellectual elite are formed.

These thoughtful words of Pope John Paul II prompt me to mention here my publishers – the Society of St Paul – already alluded to by Lord Longford in his Foreword. For they are surely active in these 'modern Areopagi' in every sense. Founded in Italy in 1914 by Fr James Alberione, this devoted and energetic priest drove his agile mind yet rather frail body for 87 years in the service of God. Inspired by the apostle, St Paul, he determined that his Religious Order would spread the word worldwide by the means of printing and publishing.[2]

On his death in Rome in 1972, Pope Paul VI paid this tribute to the Superior General of the Society of St Paul, tell the members of his Society to be faithful to him, follow his example, continue his work with the same spirit of faith. This the Pope enjoined on all.

Today in many countries, as far flung from Italy, as Britain, India and the USA, the Society of St Paul has established publishing houses, and I feel privileged to be one of their authors.

The right and duty to propagate Christ's Gospel and do his will is properly prayed collectively or universally; that is to say we should not merely address our own particular interests to God in this petition – but those of others, indeed in certain respects of the whole world. I mentioned the words of St John of Chrysostom in the last section regarding this point.

Next, the prayer mentions Free Will, thanks God for this gift and asks for help in using it responsibly. Human beings are rational and therefore they are like God; created with free will and are masters over their acts.

We are to seek God and having done so cleave to him of our own free will, but the choice is ours not God's. The Holy Spirit will guide us; Christ will teach us.

If and when we sin we are abusing the freedom given to us, but if and when we do not sin, we become *ad idem* (at one) with God and are the better able to do his will. The obverse side of this coin of freedom which we possess is of course that we cannot properly blame God for the sins of the world. Nearly all the disasters, troubles, suffering, which beset mankind, are of man's own making, or due to his neglect. I say nearly all, because I believe there are occasions when we are tested and suffer because God who will redeem us needs to use us first to help share in that redemption. Such cases will be dealt with in a later chapter.

The eminent writer and Catholic, Paul Johnson, wrote recently[3] that the most important single element in religious faith is belief in free will and that we are free spirits. Specifically on the subject of prayer when writing in the *Daily Telegraph* he said that by an act of our uninhibited will we send a signal to the Creator of all existence across the infinities of time and space, and this sign is instantly received and registered. No one can take this (free will) away from us...

The preliminaries over, my extended prayer addresses the great question 'What is thy will?' And here we should pause, reflect and listen. It is one of those moments in our conversation with the Almighty when it seems most opportune to listen – which as I have already mentioned in the Introduction to this book – is an important element in prayer.

In general terms I am sure there is a two-fold answer. There are two commandments, because He has told us so. Love of God, and neighbour. They are all-embracing, expansive in scope and rewarding beyond compare in this life and the next. But if at this stage in our prayer beyond all others, we take God into our innermost confidence, then he will show us by the inspiration of his Holy Spirit what he has in mind for us – what is his will for us.

Listen to his voice in the wind or in the crashing of the waves. Consider his creation in the spread of trees, the lie of mountains, the bending grasses cropped by sheep, or in the solid painted ceilings or stained glass of great cathedrals erected to his glory. Here in all these things and many more we can find what Archbishop Laud saw as the beauty of holiness, and we can then be inspired to do his will.

You shall love the Lord your God with all... not one or two, but all the faculties for devotion are to be exercised; heart, soul, mind and strength, which means with zeal and conviction (Mk 12:30; Lk 10:27). Such a statement of adoration has already been made in the first petition 'Hallowed be thy name'. But here there is a different emphasis because there is the monotheistic addition: '...and love no other God'. We should not forget at this point of our prayer, that no other great religious leader claimed to be divine as did, as is, our Lord, Jesus Christ. None of this is to suggest that Christianity is devoid of feeling or love for non-Christians, whether they be atheists, agnostics or from other religious persuasions. That is why I have added an old prayer at this point, which is of uncertain origin.

'Let us pray for all those who know not the name of the Lord Jesus.'[4]

There is nothing faintly patronising in this prayer; in fact the opposite. It is not that numbers alone portray right or reason, yet are these people who know not Jesus legion, even if they are divided into other loyalties or none. Rather are we acknowledging their existence and praying for their salvation through our own faith.

The second commandment of love is like the first, and of equal importance: 'Love your neighbour as yourself'.

We must love all humankind. It is an exceptionally tall order, nor can it be taken lightly, or dismissed as impossible! Bearing in mind that we are imperfect, sinful, negligent, lazy, self-centred, greedy, we must simply do our level best to love, to bear no lasting ill-will, to help and to pray for all our fellow human beings, whether or not we come into contact with them and even if they are or have been our enemies. For the prayer continues, that on these two commands hangs everything: the law, prophesies, writings and sayings of our Lord and his followers.

Before I leave comment on this second commandment, I would like to question for a moment, the meaning of the last two words, 'as yourself', which in my view are often neglected. I regret to say I scarcely considered them when praying the extended prayer. Then I came to realise that the words were important, as is every precious word in the Lord's Prayer. 'As yourself' presents us with a scale by which we can measure and evaluate the command to love others.

First I found it helpful to exclude what the words obviously do not mean; that we do not have feelings of admiration for ourselves or pride in ourselves. Having excluded such vanities can we not put it this way; we should show compassion and *agapé* and joy for all, in the same way as we do towards ourselves. In other words, just as we nurture our own worth and self esteem, or just as we protect our own soul by prayer; so should we feel towards all humankind, whether known to us or not. There is after all a good reason why we should have positive feelings of goodwill towards our own being. God created us in the image of his Son and gave us the joy of the Holy Spirit. By these gifts we have become part of God. In this way we dwell in him – and most important – he in us. This mutual indwelling is *agapé* or love, which is to be shared in prayer and deed, with others, 'as ourselves'.

The extension prayer now goes into the necessary detail as the supplicant focuses upon 'all those we so dearly love and also for our enemies'. Furthermore I choose to start with enemies, and the choice is deliberate! It is the principle of grasping the nettle. It is otherwise all too easy to relegate those who are not in our favour to the nether regions of our mind, and then to dismiss them at the end of the list of those we love best, as an afterthought. I thus list X, Y and Z being those who seem to have contempt for me or mine, for whatever reason. He or she may be a sworn adversary, perhaps even someone at work, someone who harbours, or against whom you harbour, a long-standing grudge, a person who has maligned you to others, even someone who is evil. For these people we must pray, if possible by name, asking God to forgive them and pledging ourselves to forgive them. Perhaps they too would forgive and try to understand us, and reconciliation might come about. There is however a caution. Whilst we should not hate, indeed should try to find love in our hearts for these enemies, there is no obligation upon us to compromise that which is right from that which is wrong. Indeed we should be resolute in upholding the truth at all times, as well as that which is Christian and of good report.

Always of help, St Paul told the Corinthians: 'Love

takes no pleasure in other people's sins, but delights in the truth' (1 Cor 13:6).

The present Pope enlarges on St Paul's words in this way: The love of one's neighbour must always be guided by the truth about him.' He goes on:

> First and foremost love must perceive the good in another, but also see the bad – sins and defects – and according to the sense of duty it is capable of calling this evil by name and above all is able to repair it. This is the most important manifestation of love and its touchstone, its ability to repair evil in another. Such is the love of God towards us, such is the love of Christ.[5]

Here I choose to add a personal anecdote that may be helpful. It concerns the need on occasions to uphold the truth, so far as our enemies or detractors are concerned. We should 'be not afraid!' But afraid of what? Of being ridiculed, misinterpreted, disliked, even hated perhaps, for exposing calumny, untrue gossip, gross unkindness and the like.

A few years ago, someone I considered a friend of my family, did just these things to them. Instinctively I felt uneasy about this person though I could not pinpoint why. With hindsight I could have done so, and then have acted accordingly. But I didn't and was therefore wrong in allowing what happened by default. It was only many years later, I suddenly realised the wrong that was done. The revelation shocked and what the person did that was wrong had to be exposed, to prevent further harm to others; even to the perpetrator, who was then in line for considerable advancement and promotion. Indeed at that time a group of like-minded people was emerging, whose deeds needed to be exposed or prevented. The outcome in this regard was salutary, and I feel the objectives were also for the public good. Of course the whole experience was a timely reminder that we ourselves are not without sin.

A further consequence of this exposure to us as a family was a certain suffering and defamation from some quarters, which in turn had to be met as well as dealt with. Those who are prepared to uphold and stand by the truth in this way, must also be prepared to take the unpleasant consequences of their actions. All this takes a measure of courage, but eventually good prevails and a climate of peace ensues. Love is once more restored. Most importantly such is the love of God, that in this way even evil can be repaired, and his will done.

The prayer now continues, to remember all who are near to us; to our families and friends. First if the supplicant is married might he or she pray for their spouse at the same time thanking God for his gift of the blessed sacrament of Marriage.

I have taken the marriage sacrament out of the extended prayer to the fourth petition, dealt with in chapter 4, which invokes the other six sacraments; the reason being that it seemed right to mention it when praying for a husband or wife. Marriage is also different from the other sacraments in that the vows are taken between the couple concerned and God; the role of the minister appointed by the Church being to witness and to bless the sacrament. It is, like the other sacraments, a *mysterion* and gift from God, through an outward sign bestowing inner grace. Christ, as noted in the prayer by his presence at the wedding feast at Cana could be said to have blessed the state of marriage. Marriage symbolises love for his bride, the Church. This in turn invokes God's blessing upon the supplicant's marriage and more particularly relates it to the Church. In other words here is a petition by husband and wife to share – through their direct vows to God as well as their daily renewal. The supplicant is asking that their union be wrought in Christ's blood so they are inseparable (on a continual and renewed basis through prayer) unto death and beyond. Moreover they ask that this bond between them be sanctified through the merging of the blood of Christ crucified, with the baptismal water of their mutual love for one another. In this way they become one flesh just as Christ and his Church – the Body of Christ – are one.

For this reason Catholics believe it is fitting that when they marry they also receive the Eucharist so that communicating in the same body and blood of Christ, they may form 'one body' in him.

St Paul's words in his letter to the Ephesians are both succinct and beautiful:

> For we are members of his body, of his flesh, and of his bones. For this cause shall a man leave his father and his mother, and shall be joined unto his wife, and they two shall be one flesh. This is a great mystery: but I speak concerning Christ and the Church. Nevertheless let every one of you in particular so love his wife even as himself; and the wife see that she reverence her husband (Eph 5:30-33).

Before I leave this discussion on the sacrament of Marriage, the Holy Spirit (through my praying in this way) has guided me time and time again to the wonderful importance of Christ's first miracle at Cana; not only is it his first, but his mother's role in the miracle was fulfilling his destiny and proclaiming her holiness (cf Jn 2:4-5). John says: 'This beginning of miracles did Jesus... and manifested forth his glory...' (verse 11).

For this reason I am confident I have not resorted to flights of fancy in my interpretation, but have planted both feet on the ground. We live at a time when marriages are failing faster and becoming fewer. I am convinced that by emphasising the supremacy and real meaning of our Lord's first miracle (I refer to my theory that its primary meaning relates to marriage and how marriage symbolises Christ's love for his Church), Christians are exercising a true discipleship.

It is through their marriages and together with their spouses that God's people can best envisage this sacrament, as well as give an example to their fellow human beings – whether married or not – of the excellence and holiness of their bond.

Is it not true that at Cana, Christ with the help of Mary, sanctified the mystery of marriage for all time, by his miracle? Looked at from a different aspect he also showed the world very early on in his ministry, what was his ultimate destiny; something which Mary already knew from the annunciation by the angel Gabriel.

For these reasons I would consider this first miracle at Cana together perhaps with the raising of Lazarus from the dead, to be of the utmost importance and meaning. Certainly Christ's commandment of love is epitomised through marriage and clarified by Cana.

NOTES

1 See the various publications of the *Jesus Seminar*.
2 cf L. Rolfo, ssp, *James Alberione: Apostle for Our Times*, Alba House, NY 1987.
3 cf P. Johnson, *The Quest for God*, Weidenfield & Nicolson, London 1996.
4 The word 'know' in this context does not mean 'never heard of', but 'do not acknowledge His divinity'.
5 Pope John Paul II, *Cross the Threshold of Hope*, Jonathan Cape, London 1994.

CHAPTER 4

Give us this day our daily bread

The Fourth Petition

The first of the 'us' petitions – the request for our daily needs – is also the best opportunity we have to thank God for his wondrous gifts.

The Greek word *epiousios* (daily) suggests that which is needful for the day. It occurs nowhere else in the New Testament and can be literally translated as super-essential (*epi-ousios*). If we treat it in this literal sense, then what is being given to us on a regular (daily) basis, is in fact the spiritual (or super-essential, which could mean here 'supernatural') food of the Eucharistic feast.

St Augustine has this to say:

> The Eucharist is our daily bread... so that gathered into his body (in him, with him, through him) we may become what we receive...our daily bread' (cf *CCC* 2837).

We should therefore consider this petition in its petitionary sense as a request for both our spiritual and material requirements. Bread is supreme in each regard. As a spiritual need it is the Eucharistic 'body of Christ', whilst materially it symbolises the stuff of life, the staple diet and the *sine qua non* of man's diet.

When therefore we consider Jesus Christ as he was and is – the perfectionist and idealist – how perfect and ideal that he should have us ask God each day for these and all his gifts.

Some may be perplexed as to why the word 'daily' is used. To me such puzzlement is surprising. Since the *Pater Noster* is unquestionably the most comprehensive of all prayers, it is surely worthy of man's daily use. It hardly makes sense to ask – and thank – God for something so frequently needed on a weekly basis! Just the opposite; the Our Father is meant as a daily prayer and the strange word *epiousios* confirms this. This petition above all others shows us that it is to be prayed on a regular basis of renewal. Every day, in this sense, is to be a feast day.

Prayers of petition for life's necessities or pleasures are not very important. They are secondary prayers, but neither are they to be considered unworthy since they acknowledge that the 'good things' of life are only in God's gift.

Once more in this petition as in others, the supplicant should be concerned to pray for all mankind and not merely for herself. It is no accident that the words translate as 'give us' and not 'give me'. We must show concern which is love, for the material as well as the spiritual poverty which befalls so many of God's people. Furthermore this 'us' petition coupled with 'daily bread' becomes a call for the unity of the people of God.

Pope John Paul II spoke these words at Fortaleza in Italy in 1980, and I pick out the two sentences that when written by him (as often is the case) he had underlined for greater emphasis.

> ...at the holy table all differences of race or social class disappear... thus the Eucharist becomes the great instrument of bringing men closer to one another.

I could find no more poignant a summary, nor a more comprehensive one to this petition than that written by St Peter Chrysologus:

The Father in Heaven urges us as children of Heaven to ask for the bread of Heaven. Christ himself is the bread who: sown in the Virgin, raised up in flesh, kneaded in the Passion, baked in the oven of the tomb, reserved in churches, brought to altars, furnishes the faithful each day with food from Heaven (cf *CCC* 2837).

Lest we be in any doubt as to the spiritual petition to receive Christ in this daily petition, I feel it may be helpful to recall Jesus' own words, as recorded in the Fourth Gospel, 'I am that bread of life...' and again:

I am the living bread that came down from Heaven. Whoever eats of this bread will live forever; and the bread that I will give for the life of the world is my flesh (Jn 6:48-51).

Some of Jesus' sayings to his disciples in this chapter of the Fourth Gospel are similar to one another, though not identical. But if we skim over them for this reason it is possible to miss something in the meaning, quite apart from the beauty of the translation. In my view, bearing this in mind, it is worth going back a few verses in the sixth chapter, to discover the reasoning behind Christ's assertion that the Holy Trinity is the source of life.

Part of the crowd following Jesus took to their boats and crossed to Capernaum to look for him. After he had told them to work for the food which endures to eternal life, they not unnaturally, asked him why they should believe in him. 'After all' they told him 'our fathers had bread to eat in the desert; as Scripture says: "He gave them bread from Heaven to eat."' Jesus answered:

Very truly, I tell you, it was not Moses who gave you the bread from Heaven, but it is my Father who gives you the true bread from Heaven. For the bread of God is that which comes down from Heaven and gives life to the world... I am the bread of life. Whoever comes to me will never be hungry, and whoever believes in me will never be thirsty' (Jn 6:32-5).

Martin Luther, all other considerations apart, remains to this day an eloquent intellectual whose theses are of great assistance to our learning about God.

Luther, the prolific writer, who left us a commentary on the Lord's Prayer likens the fourth petition to everything necessary for the preservation of this life; that is, food, healthy body, wife, children, good government, peace and much more. In other words, the bread which Jesus broke for his disciples was material, but also and more importantly was his body, given for many in sacrifice. It was a Messianic meal, which means both a bodily and spiritual nutrition. In the latter and more important sense, God's word is our bread.

The Extended Prayer

May we daily receive you in our hearts and minds who art the Body of Christ, knowing that we are in you as you are part of us. We ask you daily for your succour – for all our needs. We thank you, Lord, for all your goodness and living kindness to us and to all men; for our creation, preservation and all the blessings of this life; but above all for your inestimable love in the redemption of the world by our Lord, Jesus Christ, who for the means of grace and in the hope of glory died for us and for our salvation.

I believe in God the Father, Son and Holy Spirit: the Lord and giver of life; the Holy Catholic Church; the communion of saints; the forgiveness of sins; the resurrection of the body; and life everlasting.

Lord, we thank you for your gifts of the seven blessed sacraments, being outward signs of an inward grace, which prepare us for the life eternal, and on which we may feed through faith and thanksgiving:

– *Baptism,* our entry into membership of the Church through the application of water, whereby we die and are born again in Christ;

– *Confirmation,* or reception into full membership of the Church through the laying on of hands, and the divine coming into our lives and intervention of the Holy Spirit;

– *Reconciliation/Penance,* by means of absolution through an ordained priest, whereby we have an advocate with the Father in Jesus Christ our Lord, and he is the propitiation for our sins;

Ordination, by a bishop, remembering that Jesus said to his disciples 'Go out and forgive... and whosoever you forgive so also will I forgive them';

– *Marriage,* (mentioned in chapter 3);

– *Communion/the Eucharist,* whereby from consecration to consumption of your heavenly host (the Body of Christ) we might know that we are in your living presence through partaking of your body and blood, thus to love and adore you in the presence of the people of your Church, and to thank God for his great sacrifice for our salvation.

May we here pause and recall the first Mass and Last Supper of our Lord and Saviour; who took bread and when he had given thanks, gave it to his disciples saying 'take, eat, this is my body which is given for you. Do this in remembrance that Christ died for you and be thankful!' Likewise after supper he took the cup and gave it to them saying 'this is my blood of the New Testament, which is shed for you and for many for the remission of sins. Do this as oft as ye shall drink it in remembrance of me' (cf Lk 22:17-20).

This sacrament, O Lord, is the pinnacle and the very spring of our whole religious faith and understanding.

– *Anointing of the Sick,* whereby through anointing with oil when ill or even in danger of death, we might – despite the sin and negligence of our mortal lives – yet receive your grace, forgiveness and benediction, O most merciful God.

Commentary on the Extended Prayer

The extended prayer to the fourth petition begins by remembering our spiritual requirement – treating God's gift of his daily bread as meaning the Body of Christ, changed at the Eucharist from bread, into the living flesh of Christ crucified.

If we ask to receive this body into our hearts and minds on a daily basis – as at the Eucharist we receive it into our body – then we are recognising that our Lord and Saviour is ever in us as we are in him. We should always be careful to distinguish between the blessed sacrament of Communion, which can of course only be received through the consecrated host, and this constant or daily request for spiritual union.

The prayer continues by following in outline that of the Anglican prayer book's General Thanksgiving: …for all your goodness and loving kindness …but above all who died for us and our salvation.[1]

From the majority of my life spent within the Anglican communion I believe these are some of the most beautiful and meaningful words and most worthy of inclusion when we give thanks here to God, as in this petition.

Next follows an affirmation by way of an abbreviated Credo, listing the six wondrous tenets of our faith as enumerated at Nicea.

Both the *Apostles' Creed* and the *Nicene Creed* are of equal importance. The former is 'the creed of the Roman Church, the See of Peter the first of the apostles…' (*CCC* 194), as St Ambrose tells us; whereas the authority of the latter stems from the first two ecumenical Councils in 325 and 381 AD, and remains common to all the great Churches of both East and West to this day.

Through the tenets of the Creed we affirm our faith in them and remember with joy, each one with thanksgiving. They are:

- the Trinity from whom we enjoy creation as well as redemption and comfort

- The Church with its universal succession, continuity and teaching
- the example of all the saints
- forgiveness for our sins
- the resurrection of the body
- the gift of eternal life.

The prayer now deals with the sacraments. I believe that the seven sacraments of the Church provide a spiritual food or resource which is otherwise lacking. Without a full understanding of their relevance to our everyday lives and an experience of their power, we may miss some of their deep significance.

There have been many definitions of a sacrament. The most helpful explanation I can find is that a sacrament is an outward sign of inner grace. More fully it is an outward sign instituted by Christ and productive of his inner grace. It is also a mystery, that is the saving act of God in Christ.

To give an example, in baptism the material used (matter) is water, which when administered in conjunction with words (form) produces sacramental grace. It goes without saying there must also be a true disposition by the recipient; that is faith and a desire to grow in that faith. In the case of infant baptism, the faith and desire to safeguard that faith must obviously be entrusted to the sponsors who are godparents of the infant.

It might be helpful at this stage to set down a few beliefs of the Church regarding the sacraments.

First, the whole liturgical life of the Church revolves around them. Four hundred and fifty years ago, at the Council of Trent (1547) the following text was released:

Adhering to the teaching of the Holy Scriptures, to the apostolic traditions and to the consensus of the Fathers' we profess that 'the sacraments were all instituted by Jesus Christ our Lord (cf *CCC* 1114).

As the *Catechism* of the Church explains, Jesus' words

and actions were salvific for they anticipated the power of his Paschal mystery. The mysteries of his life are the very foundations of what he would dispense in the sacraments, through the ministers of his Church.

During Christ's ministry he administered the 'powers' that were to become the sacraments as 'powers that came forth' from his body. There are three direct instances of these words used in Luke's Gospel. Once when teaching Pharisees and teachers of the law, these and others witnessed the miraculous healing of a paralysed man. The writer tells: 'and the power of the Lord was with him to heal' (Lk 5:17).

On another occasion before a considerable crowd: 'they sought to touch him for power came forth from him and healed them all' (Lk 6:19).

When Jesus healed the woman with the flow of blood, who touched, in faith, the fringe of his garment, he told Peter: 'Someone touched me; for I noticed that power had gone out of me' (Lk 8:46).

In the last 2000 years, since those days, these same powers continue to be forthcoming every second of every day, for they are the actions of the Holy Spirit at work in his Body, the Church. It is vital then that we trace the origin of the sacraments from the living Word, and the three examples from the Third Gospel are apt reminders of this. The Council of Trent again: 'Celebrated worthily in faith, the sacraments confer the grace that they signify' (cf CCC 1128).

What is more they act (the Council affirmed) *ex opere operato* – which literally means 'by the very fact of the action being performed' (cf CCC 1128). St Thomas Aquinas tells us:

> A sacrament is a sign that commemorates what precedes it – Christ's Passion; demonstrates what is accomplished in us through Christ's Passion – grace; and prefigures what that Passion pledges to us – future glory (cf CCC 1130).

The extended prayer takes the supplicant through the seven sacraments starting with Baptism. This is the sacrament of regeneration and initiation into the Church. It means death to a former life. The baptised person is literally born again into the Christian faith and emerges a new person – hence importantly with a new name. In the case of infants the child is no longer 'baby' but Primrose. If an adult the likelihood is that Constant will remain the first name but now become a Christian name as well. The baptised person is incorporated into the Body of Christ. Since Baptism is an independent adult decision, and for centuries was administered to adults, the child to be baptised must have godparents who are sponsors capable of being entrusted with God's offer so that the infant may make their own full choice when capable of so doing. It is a sacrament which can never be repeated since it confers a new nature permanently. 'I acknowledge one baptism for the remission of sins', states the Nicene Creed.

In my own case, as an example, when I was received into the Catholic Church, proof of my Anglican baptism as a child was of course accepted as would that of any other Christian Church.

St Matthew's Gospel tells us how Jesus trained his disciples to baptise. They were to baptise them 'in the name of the Father and of the Son and of the Holy Spirit' (cf Mt 28:19).

Likewise St Mark records how Jesus in a final appearance to the disciples after his resurrection, told them '...he that believes and is baptised shall be saved...' (Mk 16:16).

We must bear in mind these were adults who were to be baptised. But the message is clear to all who would be godparents; how vital is their sponsorship and with what devotion it should be undertaken.

In the liturgy of the Church we celebrate Jesus' baptism at the end of Christmas, though in fact our Lord was baptised by John just before the start of his public ministry, and some thirty years afterwards. Christ did not need to be baptised. He was and is without sin, being the Son of God; but by his baptism he achieved two goals. First and foremost he sanctified the sacrament, by receiving it himself. Secondly he thereby set an example to all human-kind, that they should be baptised in the name of the Trinity.

In the same vein, Jesus had no need to pray to God the Father, since he himself is indivisible from the Father, and is God. Did he not in this way sanctify and exemplify the Our Father?

The second sacrament mentioned in the prayer is Confirmation.

Here the supplicant thanks God for, and dwells in his mind for a few moments on this sequel to the sacrament of Baptism. For this is the sacrament which confirms and strengthens our faith and admits us to full membership of the Church. The material used is in the laying on of hands and by anointing with oil, the celebrant asking that the candidate 'be sealed with the gift of the Holy Spirit'. This is the form which produces God's grace. Confirmation was not directly instituted by Christ during his ministry, since it was only at Pentecost and after his resurrection when he appeared to the eleven that he confirmed them in this way. As John records the scene: '...he breathed on them and said to them, "Receive the Holy Spirit"' (Jn 20:22).

Thereafter biblical support is found in the practices of the apostles in the book of their Acts.

Since my own Confirmation, at the hands of Rt Rev Dr Blagden (the then Bishop of Peterborough) as a candidate at Uppingham School, followed by my recent reception into the Catholic Church by Fr David Musgrave in Constantia in the Cape of Good Hope, I can reflect over many years upon two periods of instruction. As a result I am more than ever convinced that it is through this sacrament that Christians become and have the chance to re-main fully endowed by the Holy Spirit. From that time on, the same breath that Christ breathed onto his disciples is breathed onto us as recipients of God's grace. It can be likened to a personal second coming into our lives. These gifts of comfort, guidance and inspiration are ranged at the disposal of our free wills for ever.

Further to and connected with these personal experiences, I feel I should add another, before leaving Confirmation – since to me it proves the point beyond doubt, that from Confirmation onwards in the life of a Christian, there enters a third dimension – that of the Third Person of the Trinity, the Holy Spirit.

Before and during the writing of this book, usually whilst on the slopes of Table Mountain near where I live, whilst walking with our dogs and praying, I have received inspiration as to the content of my extension prayers to the Our Father. The example which follows is not of course unique, but despite my studies I had certainly not thought of it in this way.

The inspiration told me that at our Confirmation, we should feel as the early Christians must have felt at Pentecost. For here in a sense was Christ's second coming; but as then happened, it was a gift, a mystery and a fulfilled promise, as foretold by Jesus; one that would happen to strengthen them (and all believers) after his resurrection. Now, both suddenly through the sacrament, and specifically for you or me as individuals, at a given moment in our lives; we personally experience the coming of the Spirit and are filled with his presence for the remainder of our lives.

It is good advice therefore to pray in the elements when you can, and never be afraid of the wind, in the sense that physiologically it may harm you. Pneumonia is to be avoided by putting on extra clothes if you brave the wind, or have a weak chest.

Listening to a pneumatic drill at close range for too long might cause earache or worse, but pneumatology[2] means the study or thinking about the actions and person of the Holy Spirit, and is well worth giving some time to.

A gentle breeze cooling the stifling heat, a strong wind blowing away smoke or fog, turning a windmill, fanning a fire, filling a sail, or just giving comfort to the lonely or those wary of silence. To many this wind symbolises the presence of God and will guide, comfort and inspire us. It remains an ever present reminder that we are not alone and that the Kingdom is already inherited within us, waiting to be fulfilled and consummated.

Thus I feel the Holy Spirit as the breath of God, and in the Byzantine liturgy comes this prayer:

> It belongs to the Holy Spirit to rule, sanctify and animate creation, for he is God, consubstantial with the Father and the Son …power over life pertains to the Spirit, for being God he preserves creation in the Father through the Son (cf *CCC* 703).

Reconciliation or Penance is the third sacrament mentioned. The penitent should confess all mortal (serious) sins to an ordained priest, and at the same time show genuine contrition. Absolution is then given by God, according to his promise made to mankind that he would do so. Catholics are recommended to receive this sacrament at least once a year if they feel it is required. However asking for and receiving God's absolution is not to be taken lightly or for the sake of the penitent's ego. Like all sacraments, Reconciliation is a liturgical action. It consists of a greeting from the priest, a reading and an exhortation to repent, the confession with details, the imposition of a penance and its acceptance; the priest's absolution, and finally a prayer of thanksgiving and praise. The full title of the sacrament is that of Penance and Reconciliation. The sacraments of Reconciliation and Ordination are linked to an extent, when one considers Jesus' words to his disciples to go out into the world and forgive, and the injunction 'whosoever you forgive, so also will I forgive them… (Jn 20:23).

It seemed moreover an opportune time for the supplicant to remember the words of St John: '…we have an advocate with the Father, Jesus Christ the righteous; and he is the atoning sacrifice for our sins' (1 Jn 2:1). This is a constant reminder that Jesus himself absolved sinners on many occasions during his ministry, and continues so to do through this sacrament.

The fourth sacrament in the extended prayer is Ordination.

The word *Ordinatio* means ordination into an Ordo, hence the word 'Orders'. The sacrament is here conferred by a bishop by the laying-on of hands. Bishops being the successors of the apostles are those who hand on the gift of the Spirit, which is the apostolic line. Men of faith who believe they have God's call to receive Holy Orders, must submit their desire to the Church's authority, who then has the responsibility to call them.

Returning for a moment to Christ's exhortation to his disciples to forgive, was he not delegating his own divine powers of forgiveness to those twelve men in who he had placed his complete trust, whom he had ordained to minister the Word of God? By the ongoing and universal tradition of Holy Church the mystery or sacrament of Ordination thus becomes so understandable. In each of the sacraments, bar Marriage and Baptism, God's grace is channelled through the grace given the priesthood.

For the reasons given in the last chapter it was con-venient to include the sacrament of Marriage there, so the supplicant merely remembers that, at this stage in the prayer.

Communio or the Eucharist is next dealt with. From the Greek word meaning 'to give thanks', the Eucharist, or *Communio* to give it its Latin name, is the sacrament instituted by Jesus to celebrate the consecration of bread and wine, which thereby become the body and blood of Christ. The celebration of the Mass is therefore a mem-orial or re-presentation of the sacrifice offered on the Cross for the salvation of mankind by the redemption of his sins. Put another way it is, to quote an ancient liturgical for-mula 'in union with his most holy sacrifice at Calvary'.

Catholics as well as many Anglicans and other Chris-tians believe that the change wrought by the consecration of the bread and wine could be expressed by the notion of transubstantiation, so that those substances truly turn into our Saviour's body and blood, although the erstwhile physical properties of the bread and wine remain the same. Since Christ cannot be divided, this means he is totally present as God and man in either form of the sacrament. This presence occurs from the moment of consecration of the elements, until its consumption. Thus of course Christ is also present in churches apart from during Mass, whilst the consecrated host is reserved in the church's tabernacle. Faith and thanksgiving are thus vital elements of our liturgical worship during the Eucharist, but a third element which should never be overlooked is adoration.

Cardinal Hume, Archbishop of Westminster, in a book about *Being Church in Today's World*,[3] writes that adoration of our Saviour during the Mass and thus in the presence of the laity ought to be a powerful force at work. We show this adoration through prayer, contemplative or said, as well as by genuflexion and by making the sign of the Cross upon which he died. It is then, above all that we worship the King of Glory.

Pope Paul VI did much to foster what became known as the 'cult of adoration' both within and outside of the Mass reserving the consecrated hosts with the utmost care, exposing them to the solemn veneration of the faithful, and carrying them in procession.

I vividly remember as a young man stationed in Malta in the 1950's watching such processions through the main streets of Valetta, and – then as a non-Catholic – being moved by such a public display of devotion by God's people.

The extended prayer on the Eucharist ends by reminding the supplicant of its origin, at the Last Supper: the first Mass. Our Lord's words are filled with the beauty of holiness yet are they succinct in the clarity of the Divine Teacher to his disciples.

By the Last Supper Jesus gave the Jewish Passover its definitive meaning, that is the passing over of the Son to the Father by his death and resurrection.

Moreover the words 'do this in memory of me' surely remind us of the life, death, resurrection and intercession with the father, during our liturgical celebration.

The *Catechism of the Catholic Church* tells us: 'From the beginning of the Church down to our own day it remains the centre of the Church's life' (*CCC* 1342-3).

I have only recently come across these words which must no doubt have been inspired by the words the Second Vatican Council which called the Eucharist 'the source and summit of the Chritian Life' (*LG* 11), but they do confirm the final words of my extended prayer on the sacrament of the Eucharist where the supplicant prays that this mystery forms the very pinnacle of our whole religious faith and understanding. For without the sacrament of the Eucharist/*Communio* it would not be possible to adore, remember and be in the very presence of God thrice blessed and sanctified.

And so the extended prayer ends by thanking God for the sacrament of the Anointing of the Sick, the sacrament granted to us when we are ill and before we die.

Here we thank God for the compassion of his Son in his ministry of healing and forgiveness. The form of this sacrament is the laying-on of hands resulting in the gift of grace. There are so many examples of Christ's healing, body and soul. Often he touched the sick when he was man. Often the sick tried to touch him 'for power came forth from him and healed them all'. Thus through the sacraments, Christ continues to touch us in order to heal. But Jesus Christ did not always heal those who came to him; not always there and then, his healings were signs of the coming of the Kingdom of God, signs which some-times announced a more radical healing; the victory over sin and death through his Passover. Here, in other words, was a new meaning given to suffering, when in certain instances the sufferer is united with his Redeemer and shares in his suffering.[4] After all Christ's power was made perfect in weakness (cf 2 Cor 12:9).

So the anointing of the sick, and for those about to

leave this life the Viaticum through the Eucharist are offered by Church as sacraments. In the case of the Viaticum, the Eucharist is the 'passing from death to life, from this world to the Father' (*CCC* 1525).

These sacraments demonstrate to the faithful and the penitent the mercy which is beyond our human understanding, and which is shown by God to the recipient at or near the end of life; despite all the sin which inevitably we have perpetrated between Baptism and the final receiving of this sacrament.

The supplicant can play a small part in this prayer by praying for all who are in danger of death, whether we know them or not (the more so if we do) and relations or close friends of those in extremis are certainly assisting them if they can see that they receive these blessed sacraments.

May they 'look for the resurrection of the dead and the life of the world to come' (The Nicene Creed).

On a lighter note I would like to end this chapter by mention of a priest who contemplated frequently on such things:

There was a young priest
who lived almost entirely on yeast.
For he said it is plain, we must all rise again
and I want to get started at least.

On a personal note, I cannot stress too strongly the joy of belonging to the Roman Catholic Church, especially when it comes to praying this petition and giving thanks for these gifts. May I therefore pass on the following reflection by Fr Roderick Strange:

To be a Catholic is not to be loved specially, for God loves us all but it makes possible the true knowledge of that love. There is no greater gift than to be caught up in love and truth and to know it.[5]

NOTES

1 cf *Book of Common Prayer*, O.U.P., Oxford & London 1912.
2 From the Greek: pneumatikos; cf pneuma, wind; plus '(o)logy.
3 Cardinal Basil Hume, *Towards a Civilisation of Love: Being Church in Today's World*, Hodder & Stoughton, London 1988.
4 *Catechism of the Catholic Church*, para 1505.
5 R. Strange, *The Catholic Faith*, 1986, by permission of Oxford University Press.

CHAPTER 5

Forgive us our trespasses as we forgive them that trespass against us

The cardinal thrust of the fifth petition lies in the conjunction that joins what would otherwise be two sentences, if not two separate petitions. Forgive us our sins is one request; forgive our enemies is another. But Jesus did not teach them as distinct, rather as indivisible and conditional requests. The single word 'as' changes the meaning of both, so that we are asking God to forgive us, even as we have forgiven our enemies.

The unequivocal message of the petition stares at the reader at verse 15 of the sixth chapter of St Matthew's Gospel: 'If you do not forgive neither will your Father forgive you'.

Love, like the Body of Christ is indivisible. We cannot truly love God, whom we cannot see, whilst we refuse to love the brother or sister we do see (cf 1 Jn 4:20). It may seem a tall order, but the Son is not being unreasonable in asking us to pray the Father in this way. He is aware of our limitations and frailties better than we are ourselves. On the other hand, we know well enough that in our imperfections, coupled with that of our enemies, we are not expected to forget, but to forgive. Even then, this forgiveness cannot match that of our Redeemer. If we dig only a little into Scripture and at Christ's own teaching above all, then the command that we must forgive in order to be forgiven, becomes less tall. The example of God the Father through the Son is proof enough that he loves and will forgive sinners. Who are we therefore not to do likewise? If we examine just four examples of Christ's attitude towards sinners, there is proof of his infinite mercy.

These are the Parable of the prodigal son (Lk 15:31-32); his answer to Peter as to how many times we should forgive (Mt 18:22); his intercession for the prostitute who was about to be stoned (Jn 8:11); and finally in the agony of his crucifixion: 'Father forgive them for they do not know what they are doing' (Lk 23:34).

It did not mean, it does not mean, that God turns a blind eye to sin; that he does not chastise those who sin, or tell the world in no uncertain way of the wretchedness of evil and evil-doers. Yet he forgives continually, as the sacrament of Reconciliation is his blessed gift to all who seek it. Above all we acknowledge his final and supreme sacrifice in giving his only Son for our salvation, so we might conquer the sin and death and have eternal life. Through daily praying this petition and if it helps, the extended prayers to the petition, I believe it is within our reach to forgive, and thus to ask for and receive forgiveness. Some of us, and I for one, could probably do 77 times as much if I tried!

There is in my opinion a distinction between all sin generally speaking, and what we might call petty sin; and again venial sins of a more serious nature for which the sacrament of Reconciliation is appropriate. I might further speculate that Baptism is provided on account of all sins, prayer on account of little sins without which no one is able to live. We are cleansed once and for all in baptism. We are cleansed daily by prayer. Regarding the role of the Church, Saint Augustine puts it this way:

(The Church) has received the keys of the Kingdom of Heaven so that in Her, sins may be forgiven through Christ's blood and the Holy Spirit's action. In this Church, the soul, dead through sin, comes back to life in order to live with Christ whose grace has saved us (cf *CCC* 981).

Christ told his disciples 'If you forgive the sins of any, they are forgiven them; if you retain the sins of any, they are retained' (Jn 20:23).

This delegation of authority to the twelve was the forerunner of that given to Peter and the Apostles. Peter himself was the Rock on which Christ built his Church, and that Church against which even the gates of Hell would not prevail. The apostolic successors of St Peter to the present day – Christ's vicars on earth – head the Church which has, in St Augustine's words above 'received those keys'.

It is important to know there is no sin too serious which cannot be forgiven by Church, through Christ's redemption of mankind on the Cross.

Fifty years or so after our Saviour died his faithful apostle St John wrote a letter:

My little children, I am writing this to you so that you may not sin. But if anyone does sin, we have an advocate with the Father, Jesus Christ the righteous; and he is the atoning sacrifice for our sins, and not for ours only but also for the sins of the whole world (1 Jn 2:1-2).

I remember these beautiful words forming part of the Eucharistic service in the Anglican church, but then 'propitiation' rather than 'atoning sacrifice' was used, and they were known as the 'comforting words'. When I later became a barrister (or advocate) the words took on for me an added force and meaning.

The universality of Christ's suffering for humankind is

well illustrated at the Council of Quiercy in 853, when the Fathers of that Council had this to say: 'There is not, never has been, and never will be a single human being for whom Christ did not suffer' (cf *CCC* 605). He died for everyone of us that we might come to him for our salvation.

The petition on forgiveness and its reciprocal request that we forgive our detractors also merits mention in St Mark's Gospel (Mk 11:25).

In a way St Paul reverses the petition in that he first puts the need to 'be kind to one another, tenderhearted, forgiving one another', before continuing in the same verse '...as God in Christ forgave you' (Eph 4:32).

I recently re-read A. N. Wilson's excellent book *How Can We Know?* and found, as I had recollected, some considerable help in relation to praying forgiveness. In another chapter I have taken issue with Mr Wilson, but for me, his arguments and thoughts on certain aspects of forgiveness are of great value! He writes:

> ...the prayer to Our Father for forgiveness and our pursuit of the counsels of perfection go hand in hand. We cannot be forgiven if we wilfully refuse to follow these counsels. If we are ourselves incapable of forgiving we will soon lose any sense that we need to be forgiven.[1]

In other words God wants us to rely on him, who alone is perfection. He wants us to be dependent on him. We have only to try to forgive others and we will ourselves be forgiven. In the same book Wilson goes so far as to say 'Forgiveness makes higher demands upon us than if we were not forgiven', and he is right, for in order to be forgiven, we have to have made a commitment to God; there must be at least some movement towards him; some desire in our hearts. He cites the sad story of Jesus' encounter with the rich young man who 'turned away sorrowful' when told to go and sell all that he had and give it to the poor, 'then follow me' (cf Mk 10:17-22). I believe many of us have been puzzled or even upset by the apparent treatment meted out to this obviously good young man who asked what he should do to inherit eternal life. The answer he received was after all very different to that given to the lawyer. But as Wilson suggests, it was because the man turned away (without thinking) and in so doing renounced Jesus, rather than asking his help. He felt able to follow his own ideal of perfection, without reference to Jesus. Rather should he – and we – accept that Christ alone is the means to forgiveness. We have first to acknowledge that fact when we 'pray to him', 'feed off him', or find ourselves in his presence. Then as a result of our commitment, however small or imperfect it is bound to be; we will enable Christ to forgive us even as we have forgiven.

This commitment or turning to Christ is an ongoing one, throughout our lives. It does not end with Baptism, nor Confirmation, nor with the Eucharist, though these are all necessary steps along the way. God's people still retain an inclination to sin, which Tradition calls Concupiscence. This remains in the baptised so that with the help of the grace of Christ they may prove themselves in the struggle of Christian life. This is the struggle of conversion directed towards holiness and eternal life to which the Lord never ceases to call us (cf *CCC* 1426).

The Son of God who died for us that we might be saved from sin, loves each one of us to such an extent, that he needs us to find him and to seek his forgiveness – far more than we feel we need it! Let us satisfy his love for us by asking him to bring us to his grace.

I hope you will be able to follow me, when, in discussing forgiveness through prayer, claim that the importance of the *Ave Maria* cannot be overstressed. Why? Because Mary is miraculous. In every sense of the word, I stand by that statement. One of the synonyms for the adjective I have just used is 'incredible'. I bow for this information to the *New Collins Thesaurus*, and if you then refer to that word, the clouds begin to lift so that we see 'awe inspiring', 'wonderful' and 'superhuman' appearing in the list. Whereas a 'miracle' is a 'marvel'. How inspiring it might be if the intelligent editors of such work could allow themselves just one word to illustrate the faith of millions. Would 'Christlike' not be better than 'marvellous'? Let us not be distressed by my digression, although, God forgive me, I meant what I said! I return to my theme. The Blessed Virgin, Mary, Mother of God the Son, precedes our Saviour in historical fact and time, and is in the design of God the Father, the absolute precondition for his birth and ministry. At the annunciation of the incarnation of Jesus to the Virgin Mary by the angel Gabriel, the angel told her: 'Greetings, favoured one! The Lord is with you' (Lk 1:28). God, through his intermediary, Gabriel, tells Mary that he is with her, and since God is the source of all grace Mary was then filled with that grace by being in God's presence. The angel of God then tells her she is 'blessed among women' because 'blessed is she that believed'. Because of her faith, Mary becomes the mother of believers, and in effect our mother to whom we can entrust all petitions, including most importantly the present petition for forgiveness of sins. Hence we ask that she intercedes for us in our present state; 'pray for us sinners now…', and then broaden our trust to surrender the 'hour of our death' to her care and prayer. We are asking that she may be present at our death, as she was at her son's death on the Cross. Then as our Mother in Heaven, may she lead us to her Son, Jesus. As St John records the scene at the Cross: '…then he said to the disciple, "Woman, here is your son"…' (Jn 19:26).

The Catholic Church takes up St John's words: 'and from that hour the disciple took her into his own home' (Jn 19:26), and in so doing it confesses that we can pray with and to Mary, who is a sign of certain hope and comfort to the pilgrim people of God.

Christus Salvator– Homo Viator;
Christ the Saviour – Man the pilgrim.

We have to cry *mea culpa* to God in order to demonstrate that we acknowledge our sins. 'I am to blame.' The all-knowing God is of course well aware of this fact but he still wishes to hear it from us, since by our confession we are exercising the free will he has given us in his favour, and against our own sin. The other question people often ask is why, in the first place, has God – if he be all-powerful and all good – allowed sin to occur at all? He could have created us without sin and the world without crime or selfishness or hate. St Thomas Aquinas answers this question thus:

> There is nothing to prevent human nature's being raised to something greater, even after sin; God permits evil in order to draw some greater good (cf *CCC* 412).

St Augustine in similar vein tells us that God causes good to emerge from evil itself. Perhaps the best example of good coming from evil is the execution of the Son of God, which brought about the glorification of Christ, as well as our redemption. Hence the words that we sing in the *Exsultet* during the Easter Vigil: 'Oh happy fault which gained for us so great a redeemer.'

Another of the truly great saints, Catherine of Sienna, said that everything comes from love; all is ordained for the salvation of man. God does nothing without this goal in mind (cf *CCC* 313).

The Extended Prayers

Lord Jesus Christ, Son of God, have mercy on me a sinner.

Lord forgive us all our sins and wickedness which we from time to time most grievously have committed, by thought, word or deed against thy divine majesty. The burden of them is intolerable and the memory distressing to us. Absolve us most merciful Father we beseech thee according to thy promise declared unto mankind, in Christ Jesus, our Lord.

Lord have mercy upon us, Christ have mercy upon us, Lord have mercy upon us. *Kyrie eleison. Christe eleison. Kyrie eleison.*

Let us remember that we must also forgive those who have sinned against us, and that your words in this regard are repeated in the prayer you yourself taught us.

Help us O Lord in our frailty and imperfection. For thy forgiveness is complete; they mercy infinite. Though ours be imperfect let it be our best. Help us thereby to turn injury into compassion, as you do for us.

Hail Mary! Full of grace, the Lord is with you. Blessed are you amongst women, and blessed is the fruit of your womb, Jesus. Holy Mary, Mother of God, pray for us sinners now, and at the hour of death. Amen.

Here let us pause to contemplate some of the wrongdoings of the day – whether sins of commission or omission – and ponder; if they be mortal sins, difficult as they are for someone who is genuinely trying to follow Christ to commit, we should then confess them to a priest according to the sacrament of Reconciliation.

Summary of the Extended Prayers

The first of these extended prayers is the short and traditional 'Jesus Prayer', as it has become known. It is both succinct and contrite.

The next prayer is the basis, though in shortened form, of the General Confession in the Anglican Communion.[2] It is both familiar to me and as with so much that is found in the *Book of Common Prayer*, it contains a beauty beyond compare.

Next comes the thrice repeated Kyrie and Christe Eleison, both in English and Greek.

After this a reminder of the reciprocity of forgiveness and its source.

The penultimate prayer speaks for itself, but reminds us of the obvious and comparative distinction between God's mercy and our own.

I end with the *Ave Maria*, which I find, in common with so many, the most poignant intercession.

There follows a short time for contemplation, so that the supplicant can examine his or her wrongdoings of the day with God listening and understanding.

NOTES

1   A. N. Wilson, *How Can We Know?*, Penguin, London 1986.
2   cf *Book of Common Prayer*, O.U.P., Oxford & London 1912.

CHAPTER 6

And lead us not into temptation

In St Matthew's Gospel, in the Garden of Gethsemane, prior to the betrayal by Judas Iscariot, Christ addresses the kernel of this sixth petition.

'Watch and pray that you enter not into temptation' (Mt 26:41), he tells his disciples, having found them asleep as he prayed at this crucial hour. Even as he remonstrated with them he understood their failure, and told them their spirit was indeed willing, but their flesh was weak. In other words, perhaps, there is a thin dividing line between strength and weakness which can lead to sin.

Then we do well to look to St Paul, who summarises the petition wonderfully well in his first letter to the Corinthians:

...God is faithful, and he will not let you be tested beyond your strength, but with the testing he will also provide the way out so that you may be able to endure it (1 Cor 10:13).

Again later on in the same epistle: 'Keep alert, stand firm in your faith, be courageous, be strong' (1 Cor 16:13).

Vigilance then is the watchword that our Lord seems to have in mind when he tells us to pray this petition. He had to battle against temptation at the outset of his ministry, and by prayer he overcame. The story of Christ's temptation in the wilderness reflects a timeless scenario that faces men and women through all ages. At some stage in our lives, and probably more than once, we will face and have to deal with temptation. When this happens we do not have to meet the 'anti-Christ' or the 'Tempter' full on, although it may well feel like it. Our conversation for dealing with evil or sin, like his, will be a monologue conducted in our minds. We may well even play the devil's advocate.

There is temptation for all human beings to become rich at the expense of, or without caring for those less fortunate; whether in material ways or through intellectual prowess or by physical advantage.

Secondly, if you are the Son of God, do something ultra-dramatic in order to prove it, such as saving yourself.

Thirdly, the temptation to seek 'political' power at any level, from the heights of government, to domination over ones neighbour for the sake of aggrandisement. Says the Tempter: 'All these things I will give you, if you will fall down and worship me' (Mt 4:9).

May I interpret the Temptation thus: all these benefits are possible or attainable (barring number two for anyone but God) so long as you renounce God, or (if number two applies) renounce any pretension to be the Son of God. The Son of God did not comply with the Tempter, neither in the wilderness, nor at his final agony. The people of God however and those who 'know him not' are continually at risk; the former may be more so, since they at least are aware whilst the others may not be.

St Paul tells us many times in the Epistles how the Holy Spirit tries to alert us to 'keep watch' or be vigilant as in a battle (cf 1 Cor 16:13 mentioned above); so even to the end of our earthly life the petition asks for final perseverance. This means we must continually strive to remain in a state of grace, and keep the faith.

When a boy at boarding school in mid Wales (where we were evacuated during the war), I found something said by the Vicar of Llanidl oes (Rev M. E. Alban) in the course of an Anglican prayer, to be rather amusing. What he prayed included the words, 'Lord prevent us in all our doings'. My Latin at that age was insufficiently advanced to recognise the verb 'prevenire' (to go before) and irreverently I imagined God thwarting and preventing the maths master in his efforts to impart his knowledge, or the headmaster from unduly chiding us. With a bit of extra divine intervention I prayed that the train bearing us away from our parents at the end of the holidays might even be prevented from going further than London, due to the war!

In its true meaning then, when God leads us or goes before us, as well as showing us the way, he does not allow us to enter into temptation. If by our freewill we do so nevertheless, then at least he helps prevent us from yielding to it. These last are really the two meanings of the Latin word, translated by the single verb 'lead'.

The early Theologian, Origen, reminds us that God does not want to impose good on us, rather does he hope for free beings. However he teaches that temptation has a certain usefulness, by revealing the nature of our God-given souls and thus helping s to know ourselves the better. Jesus, our Saviour, who includes this petition in the prayer taught us to pray to his heavenly Father knowing that by prayer he, the Son of God, would vanquish the tempter. 'Rise and pray…' (*CCC* 2847).

Allow me briefly to return to that passage of St Paul to the Church at Corinth which I quoted at the beginning the chapter, since I believe it holds the key that God wants to give us with which to fight temptation. I interpret the passage in this way. If you (God) have to or indeed need to, test us beyond our endurance, then give us the faith to withstand it. I regret I had never until recently read so as to absorb the last 20 words of St Paul's verse. Indeed it was only after puzzling for a long while with the words of the petition itself, that I wrote down the words I have given above, which seem to explain the matter.

The main reason why I believe we can ask God to give us faith with real confidence, in the asking, is that he has already given us the assurance. Where? In the *Doxology* to the *Pater Noster*.

I will enlarge on this and explain it further in the course of chapter 8 which deals with the *Doxology* (so-called) and its importance. For now let me say we have no need to fear being led into temptation because God's is the Kingdom, no one else's; because God's is the power, no one else's; and because the glory belongs to God alone; to no one else.

The *Doxology* aside, the petition touches on the vexed but essential question of suffering. So many Christians are seriously disturbed to know how our loving Saviour can permit terrible suffering. Many atheists and some agnostics use this quandary to question the whole Christian ethic of love and to question Christ's teaching. It therefore becomes of vital importance that Christians try and answer this question, both for their own faith, and so they are able better to proclaim the faith, as is our duty to do. Of course suffering is often the result of man's freewill, given him by God, and thus cannot be blamed on God!

To give two rather absurd examples – suppose you shout obscenities at a fellow drinker in a crowded bar, and as a result receive a blow to the face from that person's broken and jagged beer glass, your suffering from such an injury can hardly be ascribed to the will of God. Likewise if an intelligent business woman makes a high risk investment on the 'futures' market, which results in her losing her entire capital, no one should say that was God's will. Sometimes however, we may be tested, which is another way of saying our faith is tested, when we encounter suffering. A chance fall on a slippery floor by an elderly person often results in a broken hip which in turn, for one reason or another, sometimes leads to death.

Let me briefly enlarge on this scenario, which unhappily is not uncommon. Suppose the victim of the fall is a Christian, baptised, confirmed, married, widowed. She has received the sacraments, prayed, loved and believed. Now she is more or less alone during her end time. But why this woman? She is deserving, surely, of God's compassion not his wrath? In fact though, it is not his wrath that has intervened, neither is her Redeemer careless of her plight. Very likely, within 24 hours of her fall, the widow prayed the Our Father, and asked God not to test her beyond her endurance. But did he? Or had he in her special case given her the faith she needed. Had she already known in part, but would now understand fully, through her God-given faith (cf 1 Cor 13:12).

The *Catechism of the Catholic Church* puts it this way: 'Faith makes us (experience) in advance, the light of the Beatific vision, the goal of our journey here below...' (*CCC* 163). So if our experience of suffering in any of its forms shakes our faith; even becomes a temptation against it, God will surely understand, but will expect us to be vigilant in prayer. In this way, as he overcame suffering and death itself, so may we. In this way we 'die in Christ', when our time comes, and we share then in his resurrection. It is also possible, I believe, that some of God's people may be called upon to share in his redemption. Such people would then be truly in him as he is in us.

This aspect of the meaning of suffering, which is really a mystery has to be considered with caution, but perhaps it is not so very hard to understand how it could happen. If for example tragedy strikes young children, it may be that they – as well as their loved ones who bear a terrible burden – in this terrible occurance not willed by God can yet somehow unite themselves to Christ, who underwent suffering for us.

How often has the following true illustration occurred? Sadly very often. The parents of one of my own godchildren (my godson lives) lost their elder child in a car accident at the age of twenty. I wrote to them as a young man myself; haltingly at the time, yet sure in my own conviction that their son who was a policeman was assured in Christ. But his parents were burdened, even crippled for a while, although they showed remarkable courage as so many do. In some way they could unite themselves to Christ in his suffering and share his burden and his redeeming grace.

The Extended Prayer

Lord help us in our earthly lives to prepare for suffering and guard against sin.

Go before us Lord Jesus and save us from temptation.

If you need to test us, let it not be beyond our endurance.[1]

And if we stumble, give us the faith to withstand the test that awaits us.

May we never falter in our love of you.

Let your Holy Spirit guide and comfort all your people and help us to be vigilant as we approach the end time of our lives on earth. Be this swift or long-delayed, save us from despair and give us hope.

Deliver us from uncertainty and grant us faith.

Preserve us from hate or apathy and grant us your peace. Amen.

Note on the Extended Prayer

Unlike some other chapters, the extended prayer to the sixth petition is short and speaks for itself. It thus requires little if any commentary.

The prayer stresses suffering and sin. We ask God to prepare our hearts and minds for the inevitability of some of each. Whether by God's testing of us, or through man's sin or freewill, both are bound to occur, and this we should accept. At all times we should retain our faith.

NOTES

1 For the Greek word for 'testing', the Aramaic idiom would be 'Do not let us go under in temptation.' (cf *Interpreters Dictionary of the Bible*, Abingdon Press, 1962).

CHAPTER 7

But deliver us from evil

When writing the first draft for this book I decided for the sake of convenience and simplicity to couple the last two petitions together. It was not to be, for it later occurred to me that this would be to fudge the issue, as well as being unhelpful to the reader. True the conjunction 'but' joins the last two petitions; true also there is a similarity of content in both of them. Having said that, they are two separate subjects, akin but different. Further, if great scholars over two thousand years, including saints and Fathers of the Church have treated them separately, who was I to change so well-established an order!

Besides which, as I have tried to show in the last chapter, suffering can either be man made or beyond our control and if the latter, then such suffering or temptation is divorced from the evil (or the devil) that we ask God to deliver us from in this final petition.

Jesus Christ in his priestly prayer to the Father asks him specifically to grant us this petition. St John records this fact: 'I am not asking you to take them out of the world, but I ask you to protect them from the evil one' (Jn 17:15).

At this early stage it should again be stressed as with

other petitions, that this one is to be prayed for the world. More so than most perhaps, this petition is so very personal to one as an individual. May I be protected from evil; and there is nothing wrong in that personal request, so long as it is coupled with all of humankind. From whom or what are we asking to be saved? The answer I believe is whom not what. It is without doubt the evil one that is meant; otherwise known as Satan, the angel who opposes God, the Tempter, or the devil – from the Greek word *dia-bolos*: the one who 'throws himself across' (*CCC* 2851) God's plan and his work of salvation. This is not to mean one is imagining the devil as a person with horns and a tail, and carrying a trident. When Christ came face to face with temptation in the wilderness he was confronted by an 'inner crisis', rather than a horned monster. He had to battle with the 'inner crisis' which was inherent in the human nature he had taken. In this sense there was no dialogue or speech. He prayed to his Father and triumphed over temptation – only he was capable of this triumph.

In the course of my research for this petition I have read a fascinating new book, *The Devil, A Biography*, by Peter Stanford,[1] which traces his subject's importance throughout the Old and New Testaments, as well as giving current attitudes towards him from the mainline Christian Churches. It was in the course of this book that I saw mention of Neil Forsyth, the historian who dwells on St Paul's writings, as does Stanford, to find a perspective on the devil or evil. Forsyth says that every time Paul uses the word Satan he is referring to the opponent of human salvation and not the figure who does battle with Michael in the *Book of Revelation*.[2]

We all know that the Devil's Advocate puts Satan's case against those chosen to support the canonisation of a saint. The department or to give it its correct Vatican name –the Congregation for the Causes of Saints – is painstaking in its research before proposing certain men and women to rank as models and intercessors.

In similar vein one might ask whether the devil is in a sense God's Advocate. Is he not our inner consciousness – we who are created in God's image and likeness – acting when required as man's tempter? Does he not sound out our imperfections on God's behalf. I mean this in the sense that God is all knowing as well as all powerful. He has fought and won his battle with Satan; whereas we have not. If we accept this possibility and are drawn to act upon it, that is when we pray to our Redeemer 'Deliver us...'

Here at the end of the *Pater Noster* we are brought face to face with truth and reality, and pray for our deliverance. Mankind is flawed by original sin although by our baptism the slate is wiped clean as we die and are born again in Christ, whose name we take. Thereafter we are al sinners to a degree, but we can be protected from both sin and evil. St Ambrose puts it succinctly:

> The Lord protects you from the wiles of the devil; so that the enemy may not surprise you. One who entrusts himself to God does not fear the devil. If God is for us, who is against us (cf *CCC* 2852).

These last words are truly comforting and wise. May I draw a figurative parallel between the last sentence of St Ambrose and criminal law with which I was involved for many years as both barrister and judge. There were times, appearing for a defendant in a criminal trial when either gradually or suddenly during its course the jury became sympathetic to one's defence. By their collective reaction it was apparent that they had heard enough and were minded to acquit. The judge however, wiser maybe and more cynical, did not always entertain this sympathy. But since despite the judge's summing up, the jury alone would have the authority to decide the verdict, the phrase was often on our lips: 'If the jury's with us who cares about the judge!' And when God is for us, as Ambrose said, who can be against us?

Hardly surprising then, the words of Christ himself, be not afraid (cf Mt 28:10).

They were the first words of John Paul II at his inaugural appearance to the crowd assembled in St Peter's Square and the title of a recent book about him. For if God is with us, nay more than that, in us, as well as loves us – and we believe in him – then how can the evil one harm us. But by prayer and vigilance we must let God hear us express our freewill to this effect.

Can there be any doubt that if we follow St John's Gospel, Jesus Christ won victory over the prince or ruler of this world at the hour when he freely gave himself up to death? He told those close to him not to be afraid. He said, 'I will no longer talk much with you for the ruler of this world is coming. He has no power over me...' (Jn 14:30).

When Jesus told the disciples that the hour had come for him to be glorified, he went on to explain: 'Now is the judgment of this world; now the ruler of this world will be driven out' (Jn 12:31).

When praying this seventh and last petition we are asking to be freed from all evils, whether past, yet lingering in our minds, from those currently trying us, or those that will assail us in the future and at our end. These include the differing trials facing all men and women that are born of evil, as well as the distress which faces the world at large; in other words and for example from calumny and corruption to war and famine. From whatever it may be – Good Lord, deliver us!

Since it is very much an 'end-time' petition, and not by chance but by design the last one, I feel we must steel ourselves and look ahead to when our earthly lives are ending, when we pray it. This means we must not be too presumptuous at the age of 20 into thinking we will not die before the age of 80! Without undue paranoia or fear it is only right to be vigilant. 'From a sudden and unforeseen death, deliver us O Lord.'[3]

As we grow older and the expectation of life becomes shorter, so much more should we treat this petition as one of hope and faith in our coming salvation. Hope we must have that our prayer will be answered, so that we may die in peace to live again for ever in the certitude of Heaven. Above all we need faith to believe that life does not end with death and that we are capable of conquering death as Christ did, through the gift of his redemption.

However hard we try there are times – and a nearness to death may well be one of them – when we can easily succumb to being 'of little faith' and be filled with a very natural uncertainty and anxiety.

We as Christians may face a bitter mind-battle with the 'anti-Christ' as to whether death will not after all obliterate us forever, despite our previous shield of faith. Or it may just be that we are filled with the fear of the sins we have committed, and which make us afraid for the erstwhile expectations we had of resurrection.

Be not afraid! Pray for deliverance from evil. God will not run away from us after all he went through to save us. We must hold on to logic as well as faith! Above all, let us take heart for the very good reason I will give in chapter 8.

For the Our Father is not yet ended – not quite!

The Extended Prayer

Dear Lord, help us to renounce the devil and all his works, for he is no more than 'the fiend that walks close behind us' in Coleridges's *Ancient Mariner,*[4] none other than the shadow of sinful man himself.

Let us know him as the ruler and prince of this world, who has no jurisdiction in the next.

Give us the ability to realise that evil in this world must exist, for the gift to us of God's freewill to exist and flourish.

We cherish that gift to us O Lord. We thank you for making it meaningful, and granting us the choice to follow you.

Deliver us O Lord, from every evil and grant us your peace, so that aided by your mercy we might be free from all sin and protected from all anxiety, through the love of our Saviour, Jesus Christ. Amen.

Note on the Extended Prayer

The final extended prayer to the petition is based on the priest's prayer in the *Order of the Mass* which comes after all have prayed the Our Father. For these requests we throw ourselves on God's mercy and invoke his gift of salvation.

The earlier concoction aims at putting the devil into proper perspective and thus taking the sting from his tail!

It ends by thanking God for his gift of freewill, which without the alternative choice of sin, would be a sham.

In the end it is well to remember the words of St Rose of Lima: 'There is no ladder to Heaven other than by the Cross.'

NOTES

1   P. Stanforth, *The Devil: A Biography*, Heineman, London 1996.
2   Cf N. Forsyth, *The Old Enemy*, Princeton 1987.
3   Roman Missal, Liturgy of the Saints.
4   'Like one that on a lonesome road doth walk in fear and dread/And having once turned round, walks on./And turns no more his head;/ Because he knows a frightful fiend/Doth close behind him tread.' *The Rime of the Ancient Mariner* – Pt VI. *Complete Poetical Works of S.T. Coleridge* (ed. E.H. Coleridge), The Clarendon Press, Oxford 1912.

CHAPTER 8

For thine is the Kingdom, the power and the glory, for ever and ever

The *Doxology*

I closed the previous chapter and the last petition 'But deliver us from evil' by stating that the Our Father was not quite ended. So far as the liturgy of the Catholic Church is concerned this is not strictly accurate, as the doxological words above are not included in the prayer, although they are mostly appended and said a short while later during the Mass. In the Didache[1] the words are as follows: 'for yours are the Kingdom, the power and the glory for ever'.

I firmly believe that the liturgy of the Anglican Church is both correct and helpful when it includes the so-called *Doxology* at the end of the *Pater Noster*. I use the words 'so-called' not to demean the Greek word *doxa*, meaning glory, but because the words 'for Thine' to 'Amen' are on a par with being glorious. They do far more than merely praise, in a liturgical sense, the name of the Father. This has already been done in the first petition where the glorification rightly takes pride of place. We start by confessing the divinity of God, and glorifying the blessed Trinity, 'Hallowed be thy name'. These end-words, in my view, are directly and purposefully linked to the seventh petition; perhaps even to the sixth as well They give the entire *raison d'être* for our being able to acclaim those petitions with faith and surety. If you ask 'why?' I answer 'because…'! In fact of course the word used is not 'because' but 'for'. 'For thine is the Kingdom, the power and the glory. Amen.'

Now put the last petitions together with the above and the prayer is complete. Do not test us (by suffering) beyond our endurance, or if you have to, please give us the faith to withstand it. But let us entrust ourselves to you (God) so that at our end we may not fear oblivion (the evil one) or damnation. We ask these things because we know and believe that yours alone is the Kingdom, yours alone is the power and yours alone is the glory. Amen! Do you see the sense and the strength of these last petitions when one prays the *Doxology* in with them? Is it not like St Paul urging us to put on the whole armour of God when we come face to face with evil and suffering and death? If God is with us in these trials, then how can we tremble at any thing, except the awe of his overpowering love (Eph 6:11ff).

I remember my first job, before doing National Service in the Royal Air Force, and after taking the Bar final exams. It was a term's teaching at my old prep school in Sussex. I had a class of eight-year-olds and thought I would gently shock them by writing on the blackboard in large letters 'God is awful'. It had the desired effect. There was a silence and then a few of the braver boys said, 'Sir, how could you write that?' I see or hear from one or two of them today, now in their early fifties, and they still remember it! *The Oxford Dictionary* tells us awful means worthy of profound respect, reverential.

Once Christ had overcome death and evil by his resurrection and ascension and also by his reappearances on the road to Emmaeus and elsewhere, and his coming through the Holy Spirit, he proved beyond doubt to Christians certain things. He established that the 'anti-Christ' had no kingdom bar a tenuous one on earth; likewise evil had no lasting power beyond the grave, and finally the glory of his triumph belonged absolutely with the Triune God.

Now is the prayer that Jesus taught us ended, and if we pray it to the end in this way with the *Doxology* included then it will continue to replenish our faith and love and hope of being in him and with him for evermore.

I return to the writer of the final paragraph of the *Catechism of the Catholic Church* for the last word – . 'By the final Amen we express our fiat concerning the seven petitions: "So be it"' (*CCC* 2865).

Wherever I saw it and whoever said that the *Doxology* is a paean of praise, is absolutely correct. Moreover I like the word 'Paean'. It reminds me of that emotive hymn composed by Beethoven, epitomising our reverence of God.

I see it as vital to our summation of a glorious prayer. Let the mind and heart soar in praise of Jesus Christ.

NOTE

1   In fairness to the Catholic Church (as I had imagined; so I find!) the Didache (8,2) does contain the *Doxology* as part of the Our Father. Further, in the Apostolic Constitutions (7, 24, 1) the words 'the Kingdom' are included with the power and the glory. Note also that the *Doxology* speaks of an existing state of present experience '...for thine *is* the Kingdom (cf CCC 2760).

CHAPTER 9

Amen

So be it! We agree. It is certain. But what do we agree? What is certain? So be what?

In the course of this last chapter I would like to deal with some answers – as I see them – to this final question. For when the background to prayer is considered, after the seven petitions of the *Pater Noster* have been examined, and the *Doxology* discussed and now that the ways of salvation and the choice before us of disillusionment or 'triumph' is clear: what is left?

The one Amen occurs at the end of this great prayer, as with all prayers. We sing it at the end of hymns, and we announce it to the priest or Eucharistic minister who offers us the body and blood of Christ. Anybody who has sung or heard the great Amen chorus which concludes Mozart's *Requiem*, and which uses this one word hundreds of times, over and over again in all four voice parts, will appreciate its magnificence and wonder at its certainty.

Amen is not only the epitome of concision and the flagpole of finality, both of which are important, it also speaks of certainty. This I believe is what the word conveys in Hebrew. Rather than certainty however I would prefer the word faith. After all if you are certain about something, you have faith in your assertion.

We have faith in Heaven when we assert in the preamble to the first petition, 'Our Father who art in Heaven...' We pray in the third petition, 'Thy will be done in earth as it is heaven'. The whole object and tenor of the prayer is eschatological. The annunciation by Gabriel is the beginning of the end. The crucifixion of Christ is the decisive initiation of the end. Within the 33 years of his life, is encompassed the beginning and the end.

Towards the end of Jesus' life on earth comes his three-year ministry in which he introduces his disciples to his and their heavenly Father, from whom he has come. Through his teaching and in his sayings and by his miracles he demonstrates his divinity as the Son of God, and foretells how he will shortly die and rise again for man's salvation. So often he tells his hearers how they may follow him and attain everlasting life in Heaven. God's will must be done; as it is in Heaven so let it be in earth, and everywhere else. Thus is the Kingdom established. Thy kingdom come. And now it is up to mankind and to each individual to bring it to fruition; to fulfil his or her personal *parousia*, towards her or his beatific vision in Heaven.

To those who were his apostles, knew him personally and came to recognise him as the Messiah, he also prepared them for his departure ahead of their own. Again he foretold, and later at Pentecost he fulfilled his promise to send the Holy Spirit. The Counsellor was to remain amongst them – as well as with us today – he who is the Third Person of the Holy Trinity.

For what purpose he had come again, he makes clear, since at Pentecost for the first time the Trinity is fully revealed, and from then on, the Kingdom announced by Christ, has been open to all believers. From that day the Spirit causes the world to enter into the last days. We have already inherited the Kingdom that has come, in order that it may be consummated. But there have to be a few fundamental conditions. The purpose of the Triune God is now completed; one God in Three Persons. The mystery and dogma of the Trinity is explained and confirmed by various Councils of the Church, from Nicea (325) through Constantinople (381), to Toledo[1] (675) and Florence (1439), and enhanced again in our own times by Vatican II.

For me and I hope for you, the words of St Basil concerning the gift of the Holy Spirit are most comforting and rewarding:

> Through the Holy Spirit we are restored to paradise, led back to the Kingdom of Heaven and adopted as children, given confidence to call God 'Father' and to share in Christ's grace, called children of light and given a share in eternal glory (cf CCC 736).

Thus is Christ's mission brought to completion by the Spirit in the Church, which is both the Body of Christ and a dwelling place of the Holy Spirit. And again we say Amen at the end of the Creed. Yet our mission as part of Christ, and members of his body the Church, is not yet complete, for at the end of our earthly life, we must if we so choose consummate the Kingdom of Heaven which we have inherited.

We know the way. Christ gave us explicit instructions. As for finding an unfamiliar way in the dark, I am often very stupid; everything appears to be different in the dark. But Christ told Thomas quite clearly: 'I am the Way'. With these instructions can you go wrong? Thus through our faith we know the way; and how best may we describe that faith? Again, for me the answer lies in what Jesus said to Thomas (according to St John) eight days after his appearance to the other disciples, in what I have called his coming in the Holy Spirit. On that next appearance Jesus invited Thomas to place his hand on our Saviour's crucified side, saying '...do not be faithless but believing'. Thomas answered him, 'My Lord and my God'.

Jesus Christ then spoke to all of humankind through his servant Thomas: 'Have you believed because you have seen me? Blessed are those who have not seen and yet believed' (cf Jn 20:19-29).

There are however still imponderables, despite our faith, and I mention two. The first concerns the nature of our destination; the second, about how we may function there. The first – where we are going – is both serious and fundamental. The second – what it may be like – is quite fascinating and wonderful. It is pure happiness but – and I'll come to this later – it will mean work for which we will be fitted.

The Holy Spirit appreciates these anxieties and is here *in situ*, amongst us, to help us resolve them, or at least to be aware of them. As to the nature of our destination, where might it be? Many Christians have written about it and I am sure it is both healthy and natural that they should. To a Catholic there are two possibilities: Hell or Heaven, with a variation on the latter – in that we may spend some time being 'purified' before entering Heaven. Contemporary thinkers, like Paul Johnson, consider Hell to be an unlikely destination for those who profess to be Christian.[2] For myself, I cannot envisage Hell as being what my Creator meant for me. I am a sinner but I confess him as my Christ, and love him with my fellows. I do not therefore consider myself as a candidate for Hell. It worries me however that there are people who may be destined for that terrible torment and dire punishment which we call Hell and it is surely our duty as sinners to pray continually for these souls who may be damned. Moreover my faith tells me that God will understand such a request for he is ultimate love and mercy. Perhaps that is what Pope John Paul II meant, when André Frossart, the French writer asked him what his prayer for the world was, and the Pope replied, 'I call on mercy. Yes I call on mercy.'[3] Now it could be thought that such prayer to absolve those already damned, might be contrary to God's intent that the damned shall be punished eternally in which case I can only ask for forgiveness for my lack of understanding and my presumption. I am however fortified by what St John

Chrysostom said, 'Let us not hesitate to offer prayers for the dead who may thereby be consoled' (cf *CCC* 1032).

Thus in my extension prayers for 'Thy will be done...'[4] there is also included a prayer for those in purification, that state en route to Paradise; the ante-room for Heaven. According to the *Catechism*:

> All who die in God's grace and friendship but still imperfectly purified are indeed assured of their eternal salvation, but after death they undergo purification, so as to achieve the holiness necessary to enter the joy of heaven' (*CCC* 1030).

John of the Cross speaks of a state in which some souls find themselves in this life even before death, in which the purifying flames of love envelop them.[5] Perhaps this can help us to understand the purification which we some-times call Purgatory. This being the vision of such a great mystic, then we must consider the warmth of God's love towards those in this state, as being salutary, considerate and wonderful; rather than in any way punitive or grue-some. Perhaps this state of purification can be likened to an ante-room to which men and women with near-death experiences have described. Many have told of travelling through a dark tunnel with a brilliant light at its end – perhaps hardly surprising for Christians on their way to resurrection. Thereafter variations occur, but many refer to being shown around a picture gallery in which the pictures enact episodes of their earthly lives. We must remind ourselves, these people almost died, or did so clinically before revival.

Imagine the scene (if you will allow me to speculate rather freely) – there will be those praying for the recently departed soul: 'In paradisum deducant te angeli' (May the angels lead you into Paradise). Now, one of these angels may be present to examine the newly-arrived soul. Note that I use the word examine rather than cross-examine, both terms being familiar to me as a criminal advocate.

To bring the angel into legal parlance, he or she, as I see it, is an officer of the Court, in the same way that Counsel is for the prosecution – there, if you like, to assist the soul and to assign it to its destination. Around this gallery (which contains the pictures representing episodes of their earthly lives) they progress. The purpose as I have said earlier is not to condemn, but to elucidate one's faults or sins; and not always to point to these; indeed more often, to draw attention to the good thoughts and deeds and prayers, that the newly-arrived soul has experienced in earthly life. I am sure that the point being made by those who have experienced near-death, is that their overwhelming sense was not of fear, still less of terror. Rather were they witnessing some kind of evaluation of their earthly lives. The fact that this examination-in-chief was all-embracing as well as amazingly accurate, made them marvel. Furthermore it engendered in them responses of truth and purity. No guile nor any defensive mechanism was required. A spirit of love and consequently a complete baring of their souls was prevalent and natural. This process perhaps has something in common with that mentioned by John of the Cross when he wrote 'At the eve of our life we shall be examined in our love' – though of course the Saint is referring to a time when we are still in this mortal state. It is very interesting to note, however, that the saint mentions judgement as being at the eve or end of one's own life and not at one's death or some remote day when the mass collective of all humankind that ever was, will assemble to the greater glory – one fears – of Maestro Tintoretto or others of his like.

I make this assertion with complete confidence because I have read it in the *Catechism of the Catholic Church* (*CCC* 1022); that is to say that we all receive our eternal retribution at the very moment of our death, and in a particular judgement that refers our life to Christ. It will be particular to each one of us, and not a mass or arbitrary sorting out of goats from sheep. Some may recall the old-fashioned parade in the services, when the Station Warrant Officer (in the RAF) had the audacity, albeit the duty, to ask Jews, Roman Catholics and non-conformists to 'fall out' whilst the padre recited some Anglican prayers!

What, perhaps, does the parade episode tell us about judgement? I think it is for the individual reader to make their choice here. To me, it may mean that times and interpretations change from the time when this parade took place (1955) – as it had for countless years before no doubt – and now when it would be unthinkable. In other words (but I do not want to be specific here) judgement day (in the general or final sense) is far from simple.

As a result of this judgement we will either receive entrance into the blessedness of Heaven immediately; or after a purification, or face everlasting damnation.

The *Catechism* teaches me this, as I have said. Furthermore in converting to Christ through penance and faith, we can be assured of this. We should be greatly strengthened in our faith by hearing St John's Gospel on the matter: '...anyone who hears my word and believes him who sent me, has eternal life; and does not come under judgement, but has passed from death to life' (Jn 5:24).

Can there be anything more comforting or more unequivocal than those words of Jesus?

Now my idea is simply this. The ante-chamber which leads to Heaven may itself be Purgatory. Such a scenario would fit well with 'the purifying flames of love' envisaged by St John of the Cross.

For a normal candidate soul en route to Heaven, who was not to be recalled before the event – and I will return to that – the time involved would I feel sure, be quite irrelevant. For in the many mansions of Paradise the scales of space and time cannot be related to our earthly existence. We admit after all that the bounds of space as I have already alluded to, are such that mankind is still on the edge of forever. When it comes to time we have little conception of what it means in relation to all creation, even when scientists talk grandly of millions (or maybe trillions) of light years dividing one galaxy from another.

So far as the time scale pertaining to judgement is concerned, I do not intend to say much more than I have already. How long do we have to wait – a 1000 years? Anyway, what is a 1000 years, which in a heavenly context is more likely to be the twinkling of any eye? (cf 2 Pet 3:8) For these reasons we must not consider Purgatory in terms of time. Since the Holy Spirit will remain there, as here, with God's people who are called there, and they are assured of salvation. They have far more important tasks than to watch the clock!

Before leaving the near-death experiences, I would only ponder one more question and attempt to answer it. Why are these souls and their bodies recalled to life, after – in a way – they seem to have left it? Are they restored, as Lazarus was, in order to live longer? One possible answer is that God is using them to further his mission on earth, in the sense that they are certain to broadcast their experience, whether miraculous or not, and do so to the greater glory of God. There may well be other reasons which are not for us to know and which will remain a mystery in this life. It would certainly seem that the Christian faith of those restored to clinical life following these experiences, is wonderfully enhanced and renewed.

I come now to the last destination, Heaven. When we are finally blessed to enter the Kingdom of Heaven in its fullness and see God for ourselves, we will not be alone. For: 'Beside each believer stands an angel as protector and shepherd leading him to life' (*CCC* 336).

God alone suffices as the famous 'Bookmark' of St Teresa of Jesus reminds us, and it is only he who can provide the perfect life for humankind, and this perfection is the final communion of life and love. In this communion will be the Holy Trinity, the Virgin Mary, who was as we believe assumed into Heaven, angels and all the blessed. And these last we can assume will include loved ones – as well as enemies – of ourselves. Once we are so united with Christ, and see our Beatific vision then we have arrived in Heaven.

'For life is to be with Christ; where Christ is, there is life, there is the kingdom' (*CCC* 1025).

The journey has been rough and hard; thus we have been 'associated with his suffering as the body with its head, suffering with him, that with him we may be glorified.' These beautiful words, which I find so helpful are taken from the document *Lumen Gentium* (*LG* 4), compiled by the Second Vatican Council in 1964. But as we share in Christ's suffering and whilst we pray to him and try to do his will there is no reason on earth – and I use this phrase literally and deliberately – why we should not learn and understand more of his life's mystery and meaning. This is what I mean in my extended prayer 'May we know you more nearly, and love your more dearly, as our lives ebb' (see chapter 1 page XX).

If we do this I believe we can help ourselves and others to contemplate better his heavenly glory, which can also be ours. St Cyprian (cf *CCC* 1028) tells of the eventual glory and happiness which awaits men and women. Legion are the Saints, Fathers of the Church and other great theologians, who have by study and imagination, as well as by faith, opened doors for us to follow through. It is only in this way we can decide for ourselves and tells others about our faith. Composers, artists, writers – it matters not – are enabled in this way to add to the faith. If then we are inspired from time to time through originality of composition, style and colour or musical tone, then in turn we add something to the fund of knowledge which enriches the soul and increases the faith.

We are now at the second of my two imponderables. How will we function in Heaven. I hasten to write this is not just – though it is in part – a luxurious question to ask. Whilst we hope for glory (or Heaven) this is thought on its highest plain. Even the contemplation of it is ecstasy and worthy of our best endeavours. In other words lovers should love more dearly and writers write more fervently, to name but two! Since the next few paragraphs are about

Paradise and love, let me try if inadequately, to state a case. A few years ago I read a work of fiction, which enthralled me. Its title is *Happiness*; its author an Oxford Don.[7] Its philosophy you will have to interpret as you will; but I found it inspirational, delightful and important. Let me dwell on the last of those three adjectives for a moment. The book is pure fiction and so should not offend unless perhaps readers with high sensitivity took exception to a certain flippancy in the author's style, which nevertheless captures for me, my intense interest in humanity, whether sinful or glorified. Having said that, why should this book be important? The answer lies in its imaginative thoughts about Heaven, which to me never offended. I would however go a step further and say, even had it done so momentarily, that it would in my estimation have only been in order to stimulate religious thought and provoke Christian reaction.

In a nutshell it is the story of a young woman who enters Heaven on a temporary visa, her only companion being an insect which accompanies her in a plastic bag. The treatment of Paradise is both imaginative and original, and nowhere is there any suggestion that this is anything but God's Kingdom. There are exact replicas of everything that exists on earth. Time and space are irrelevant, yet historicity is faithfully accepted. Not only is earth reproduced in its entirety, so can the traveller visit Nazareth at the time of Christ's birth, or witness Hannibal's crossing of the Alps or spend time with Shakespeare as he wrote his plays. Possible? Yes, because these events happened. Where could there be a more faithful mirror of fact than in God's Kingdom? There all is known, nothing can be hidden and light is truth. We must never forget that fiction can be inspired – perhaps even 'divinely'. The visions recorded in the *Apocalypse* (Greek 'revelation') traditionally attributed to St John are also expressed in figurative and poetic language, which has something in common with the language sometimes used in fiction. This work is regarded as divinely inspired – though of course as Scripture we do not consider it exactly similar to fiction, however inspired that fiction may be. But perhaps this work of fiction we have mentioned can help us to understand a little more about Heaven.

I hinted earlier on in the chapter that I believe those who are bound for Heaven are also fitted for work to be done there. Let me now speculate. Whereas Heaven is undoubtedly a state of supreme bliss or blessedness, that does not mean it is a place of idleness, which in turn leads to ineffectiveness. There can be nothing worthless about being in glory with God. The consubstantial God of the Trinity does not idle time away, and resurrected souls are part of God. They live in Christ and are one with him and all the people of God in his Kingdom. So what may these souls do to work for the glory that they share and in which they are now partners?

Here you will understand I must use my imagination, and any such talents that are mine. If God can count the grains of sand which cover both earth and sea, then we humans can make some estimation of the trillions of our fellows who have inhabited the earth since the creation. The total matters not, but is massive. Suppose a great proportion of these trillions who have died or are dying, reach Paradise. It can never be overcrowded because Heaven is a state of God's creation. Neither is there crime, nor disease nor ageing, nor death which is no more. There is love in abundance, joy in plenty and work to do; which is not punitive, nor restricted, and is neither for wages nor the amassing of wealth. There are no unions, nor political parties, employers, strikes, lockouts, or the like with which mankind has so arranged its life. But there is much work to do, for which every soul is fitted and thus happy to perform. One thing is certain from all this; there is no shortage of soul power. Each person chosen for a 1000 tasks will have scope and time without end to fulfil them. All this means we have to cease to be amazed when we consider Heaven. Rather should we believe in it as love which is indestructible since it is everlasting. Moreover the

Creator of that love reigns over, yet dwells within each and every soul and body that inhabits his Kingdom.

For an earthly example of how this love of God radiates in Heaven we have only to look at the lives of those (the saints are a good example) whether priest, religious or lay, who over the centuries by their prayer and example have interceded for all in an attempt to take others to Heaven with them, and to focus God's mercy on those who suffer and sin in this world.

There must be others in different parts of the world who were similarly taught, but I remember as an English boy, being given an analogy of the power of religious prayer. It was none other than the Battersea Power Station in south London. Today the analogy would be more modern. Then it was Battersea with its yellow chimneys – designed I think by Sir Basil Spence – pointing elegantly towards the sky and giving a promise of prayer rising resolutely *ex terra* and hopefully *ad Deum*! It impressed me and I remember it and pass it on. My point is, if those wonderful people of God can dedicate their lives to our good and for our ultimate salvation, then how much more so will the souls and bodies in Heaven be fitted and used to do likewise. I believe they are able, have been able, to influence those still living and yet to be born, to opt for God. As to the means by which this can be done our minds may boggle, but they need not. Through the Holy Spirit the power of prayer is a two-way traffic. It not only flows from us to God and vice versa, but from Heaven to ourselves in the broadest sense. For the glorious company of Heaven is part of God. More than that, it is part of Christ glorified, who was made man and knows our hopes and weaknesses. We are his sheep.

I envisage, if I may speculate again, that those in Heaven can help to do God's will either on earth or elsewhere where human beings exist, along these lines. They will be able to attach themselves to the relevant Department of State, the equivalent in many countries to a Department of Foreign or External Affairs. The Curia, which is the

'Civil Service' of the Vatican, a separate State in Rome, has a better name for it. There the particular Congregation (Department of State) is called the Congregation for the Evangelization of the Peoples. A bit of a mouthful perhaps, but it means exactly what it says. The Congregations are presided over by a cardinal, but in Paradise it could also be an archangel or a saint. Under their guidance each one assigned might minister to a given number of the living. Some would I suppose be known to them and be even more helpful, but the great majority could well be unknown. In these cases, it would be similar to the times when in our daily prayers, we pray for 'all who are sick or hungry' or 'for those who have lost God and wish to find His Way again' or for all those in authority over nations...' Can you not imagine that God's Kingdom in Heaven is a powerhouse of prayer and intercession so much greater, far more effective and much more modern in its efficiency, than any effort, however noble and well intended, that emanates from earth?

Allow me now to take you with me as I enlarge these thoughts. This is the beauty and the wonder of Heaven. Suddenly (or gradually, it matters not) we see the scope souls have, to do God's work. What he wants most is to show his love for us. And how best to fulfil this love than to evangelize the same on earth and elsewhere.

Prayer and intercession are paramount. Now let me mention others. Compassion – the extraordinary way in which God manages to soothe the unsoothable – the death of a child (let alone a parent) is an example. I believe this is a task that is delegated to grandparents and others who are in glory with God.

Then there is inspiration! Did Mozart's music, Harvey's discovery of the circulation of blood, Newman's sermons or Mother Teresa's love not find inspiration from those in communion with God?

And what about love on another plain. Here one is considering the vast volume of human understanding which affects millions on a daily basis. I mean the prevention of a husband and wife, of lovers and friends, from harming the love between them in a permanent way. Then on a much lower level, but to mortals most frustrating – losing things! Perhaps it is age, but I do it all the time. Almost always, sooner or later, it is found; and 'thank you God' I say. Even if there is no limit to his love; here is a task he delegates to all who live with him.

Next, let me include all those for whom we pray in the third petition and for whom the heavenly host must be even more effective – those who cry for *hope*. I mean the spiritually desperate, the poor and homeless, the hungry, agnostics, atheists, those awaiting trial or prisoners, and of course, the seriously sick. These and others whom I have failed to mention, number countless millions on this earth alone. Imagine here the scope for delegation, and the work that's done.

Last, and maybe most important, is the need to impart *faith*. Here the sheep are numberless; but so are the shepherds. Steeped in love and clothed in hope, this heavenly host is also armed with faith; the very weapon that they need to save those that will be saved.

Twenty years ago, when I prosecuted for the Metropolitan Police (London's police force) a brilliant recruiting poster for the force proclaimed, 'Dull it isn't!' The Commissioner and his advisors realised they needed more officers who were prepared to lead a life which was more often than not exacting, seldom materially rewarding and sometimes dangerous. Likewise Christians are urged to proclaim their faith, recruit more of God's people for salvation while realising that this life is not always easy. But the main message from God to us contained in the Lord's Prayer in my view is about our *salvation*. Christ came, Christ taught… so that we might all be saved and given eternal life in him. And it will not be dull for those who do God's work in Heaven. But they also have another and far greater dimension: they live with God in his glory, so that, thanks alone to him, they have become not only his children, but transmit his love to others.

As I mentioned earlier, life on earth is full of mysteries some of which we may fathom and others which we may never completely understand. Perhaps we are not meant to, until all things are revealed to us in the life eternal.

Some of these mysteries, whilst not fully explicable, carry divine messages. Miracles, visions, appearances are obvious examples. Often the saints and equally other holy men and women have been endowed with unworldly powers such as bilocation,[8] and revealed these gifts on earth in order to spread God's word amongst receptive people. It also follows that man being sinful for whatever purpose, may contrive such gifts, either to mock God, or more often for his or her own dishonest purposes. It behoves us to distinguish between the false and the divine.

Since such mysteries are undoubtedly employed by God on Earth, and maybe elsewhere too, it strikes me that those who live with our Lord in his Heaven, may well be given work to do in such a sphere. In other words, whereas there is patently a physical divide between God's people here on earth and all the multitude of Heaven – there is no reason why this should not work in reverse. Whether by the inspiration of the Holy Spirit, or however it is ordered, I am convinced no barriers exist which would make it difficult in any way, for the souls of the faithful departed to do God's will far outside his heavenly Kingdom.

I am happy to add that all that I have recently surmised about the use we might have in Heaven, is fully borne out by the Church. This I confess I did not know until after writing the above, when I came across a section in the *Catechism*, entitled 'The Communion of the Church of Heaven and Earth' (cf *CCC* 954ff).

At the Second Vatican Council, in 1964, the document *Lumen Gentium* states:

When the Lord comes in glory, death will be no more and all things will be subject to him (at Christ's final coming). But at the present time some of his disciples are pilgrims on earth. Others have died and are being purified, while still others are in glory, contemplating 'in full light, God himself triune and one, exactly as he is' (*LG* 49).

This wonderful document, *Lumen Gentium* goes on to say that the 'union of the wayfarers with the brethren who sleep in the peace of Christ' is in no way impaired; to the contrary, it is 'reinforced by an exchange of spiritual goods'(*LG* 49).

Then continuing to confirm what I have been trying to say, *Lumen Gentium* becomes more specific. It declares that those in Heaven being more closely united to Christ, do not cease to intercede with the Father for us, as they proffer the merits which they acquired on earth through the one mediator – Christ Jesus – '*so by their fraternal concern is our weakness greatly helped*' (*LG* 49).

In such distinguished and holy company, I cheerfully give thanks to the Holy Spirit for guiding me in my thoughts, and giving me inspiration in my work.

St Dominic, the founder of the Dominican Order, to whom St Thomas Aquinas belonged, made this simple and beautiful contribution to the whole subject of working from Heaven towards earth, when dying, and to his brothers: 'Do not weep for I shall be more useful to you after my death and I shall help you then more effectively than during my life' (cf *CCC* 955).

Likewise, St Thérèse of Lisieux, said when near to death: 'I want to spend my Heaven in doing good on earth.'[9]

Before I leave the matter, I promised to refer to what Pope Benedict said in 1336 – 628 years before Vatican II, which goes to show that dogma and doctrine and their interpretation are never static and retain their relevance.

Benedict begins: 'By virtue of our apostolic authority, we define the following…' He then continues in this same vein; that is with obvious certitude and faith, to endow all those who die in Christ, with the knowledge of his heavenly kingdom. He states concerning the souls of 'all the saints and other faithful', excluding those who may first need purification:

> ...before they take up their bodies again and before the general judgement – they HAVE BEEN, ARE, AND WILL BE IN HEAVEN – WITH CHRIST. Since the passion and death of our Lord Jesus Christ, these souls have seen and do see the divine essence with an intuitive vision, and even face to face, without the mediation of any creature (cf *CCC* 1023).

As I have always thought and believed, Benedict makes clear: Christ's promise to humankind is sacrosanct. Our judgement is upon our death. Once made it will not be varied. After his death and glorious resurrection – and if we are found faithful in his dual command, a general judgement will not let us fall from glory and his Kingdom. Such faithful souls – shortly to be reunited with their heavenly bodies – are forever part of Christ.

For once the faithful departed have seen Christ, and entered into the Beatific Vision, then like the thief on the next cross, they have arrived 'that day' in Heaven. Once there, there is no way in which our Redeemer will renounce them, for henceforth they live with him in Glory.

When we say in the Creed that we believe God will come again in glory 'to judge the living and the dead', what do we mean? To judge the living in this context is easier to understand; for that is an ongoing judgement and has been applied to all those now in Heaven. And when Christ should come again, then those living will be judged. But for the dead who have already been damned; this could be the final judgement. If this be so, then there is hope even for those who have already condemned themselves. I put this possibility forward in humility. Whatever is the answer to this mystery, there may be some support for what I have just suggested, in the interpretation of the theological writer William Neil who argues that God's gracious purpose is our salvation and not our condemnation. But, he continues, the choice is our own. If we chose to live in the darkness of unbelief we damn ourselves, and the final assize merely confirms judgement that we have already passed on ourselves; God is working in us.[10]

I have sometimes asked myself how God can ever personally consider the supplications that we make to him, let alone answer them himself. The answer must be that he can and does, but we tend to overlook this great company of Heaven, of which I have just written: a company which is made up of those in glory with God, even though they work through him. Consider in that context the massive and dedicated army that the King of Heaven has at his disposal, to intercede on our behalf! And be thankful. This is the company that I refer to, whose ranks we may join and whose task we shall assist.

As this last chapter, and thus the book, works towards its end, and its Amen, and since it has been a reflection about talking to God – woven around the most important prayer of all time – may I tell you about my happiest times of praying, and thus perhaps the most fulfilling.

Praying the Father daily and privately is always rewarding and a source of continual happiness.

– In great cathedrals; yes, there has been great awe and majesty.

– In one's parish church; of course the sense of belonging to the flock led and inspired by the parish priest.

– In bed with my beloved wife, when saying those few but very special words to God.

But differently, ethereally, and with a wondrous feeling of being enveloped by the power of angels, I have always felt lifted toward the love of Jesus Christ when praying – where I was received – amidst the nuns of Schoenstaat before the evening *Angelus* in their tiny Marian Shrine.

1 Here it was confirmed that the Holy Spirit is the Spirit of both the Father and the Son.
2 cf P. Johnson, *The Quest for God*, Weidenfield & Nicholson, London 1996. I do not say these are his words, but I believe his sentiments – with which I agree.
3 A. Frossart, *Be Not Afraid*, Bodley Head, London 1982.
4 See chapter 3.
5 John of the Cross, 'Llama de amor viva' ('Living flame of love').
6 St John of the Cross, Dichos, 64.
7 T. Zeldin, *Happiness*, Collins Harvill, London 1988.
8 Supernatural gift possessed by some holy people to be in two places simultaneously. During the process of Bilocation the human body is actually duplicated through the grace of God. (See *Miracles* by D Scott, Rogo: ch. 4.)
9 From *St Thérèse of Lisieux Her Last Conversations* translated by John Clarke, O.C.D. Copyright 1977 by Washington Province of Discalced Carmelites, Inc. ICS Publications 2131 Lincoln Road, N.E. Washington DC 20002, USA.
10 William Neil, *One Volume Bible commentary*, Hodder & Stoughton 1962, 1973 Ed. (cf. Jn 3:17-21).

A short glossary

(N.B. this glossary represents my attempt to understand the various terms)

CATECHESIS 'The totality of the Church's efforts to make disciples to help men believe that Jesus is the Son of God, so that believing they might have life in His name; and to educate and instruct them in this life, thus building up the Body of Christ.' (Pope John Paul II – Apostolic Exhortation – *Catechesi Tradendae*, I,2.)

CATECHISM The *Catechism of the Catholic Church* published world-wide in 1994, based on the conclusions of the Second Vatican Council (1964-1968) 'to modernise, guard and present the precious deposit of Christian doctrine... to the faithful and to all people of goodwill...'!

DOCTRINE The affirmation of a truth, or a teaching of the same.

DOGMA A truth revealed by God; directly and formally, and therefore to be believed by the members of the Church.[1]

INCARNATION St John tells us 'in the beginning was the word and the word was God' (and later) – 'and the word became flesh and lived among us ... full of grace and truth' (cf Jn 1:1-14) Thus the Church calls the fact that the Son of God assumed a human nature, in order to accomplish our salvation – 'incarnation'.

INFALLIBILITY St Peter and the other apostles handed to the Church the Faith of Christ who is the Truth. Thus Christ in turn willed to her a share in his own infallibility. The Pope, by virtue of his office as the Vicar of Christ enjoys this infallibility, when he explicitly proclaims by a definitive act, a doctrine pertaining to faith or morals. This infallibility is also present in the body of bishops, when together with Peter's successor they exercise the supreme Magisterium, above all in an Ecumenical Council.

Several of these Councils are mentioned in the book (starting at Nicea in 325) but only since Vatican I and II (the 16th and 17th Councils 1869 and 1962 – has the doctrine of papal infallibility been defined.

MAGISTERIUM of the Church exercised in catechises and preaching, with the help of the works of theologians and spiritual authors. It thus becomes a deposit of teaching; the basis of which emanates from the Creed and the Our Father.

SACRAMENT bestows to baptised people (ex opere operato) the necessary grace proper to each of the seven gifts. The sacraments have a salvific function[3] (see also chapter 3). For a rather fuller discussion, see also chapter 4.

TRINITY The Three Persons of the Holy Trinity, God the Father, God the Son and God the Holy Spirit are consubstantial and indivisible, though God exists in these Three Persons. These Persons perform roles in the above order and are thus numbered to comply with being Creator, Saviour and Paraclete. But their Majesty is co-eternal.

To avoid anthropomorphic consideration of the First and Third Persons of the Trinity, it is helpful to see the second meaning of 'Person' in the *Concise Oxford Dictionary* (5th. edition) – 'the three... Modes of being of the Godhead...' (from Modus, L. and see also the word Modal Of mode or form as opposed to substance, from Modalis, L.).

NOTES

1 See *Catechism of the Catholic Church*, St Paul Communications/Daughters of St Paul, Nairobi Kenya 1994 and especially the foreword by Pope John Paul (p.23).
2 *Catechism of the Catholic Church*, para 461.
3 *Catechism of the Catholic Church*, para 2032 and seq.
4 D. Jacob, *Encyclopaedia of Theology*, Burns & Oates, London 1975.

Index